Con$umption
& Generational
Change

T0291233

Consumption & Generational Change

The Rise of Consumer Lifestyles

Ian Rees Jones, Paul Higgs, & David J. Ekerdt, editors

Routledge
Taylor & Francis Group

LONDON AND NEW YORK

First published 2009 by Transaction Publishers

2 Park Square, Milton Park, Abingdon, Oxfordshire OX14 4RN
711 Third Avenue, New York, NY 10017

Routledge is an imprint of the Taylor & Francis Group, an informa business

First issued in paperback 2017

Copyright © 2009 Taylor & Francis

All rights reserved. No part of this book may be reprinted or reproduced or utilised in any form or by any electronic, mechanical, or other means, now known or hereafter invented, including photocopying and recording, or in any information storage or retrieval system, without permission in writing from the publishers.

Notice:
Product or corporate names may be trademarks or registered trademarks, and are used only for identification and explanation without intent to infringe.

Library of Congress Catalog Number: 2008029437

Library of Congress Cataloging-in-Publication

Consumption and generational change : the rise of consumer lifestyles / Ian Rees Jones, Paul Higgs, and David J. Ekerdt, editors.
        p. cm.
    Includes bibliographical references and index.
    ISBN 978-1-4128-0857-6
    1. Consumption (Economics)—Social aspects. 2. Older consumers.
3. Consumer behavior. 4. Population aging. I. Jones, Ian Rees.
II. Higgs, Paul. III. Ekerdt, David J. (David Joseph), 1949-

HC79.C6.C6726   2008
306.3—dc22   2008029437

ISBN 13: 978-1-4128-0857-6 (hbk)
ISBN 13: 978-1-138-50855-2 (pbk)

Contents

Part III: International Comparisons of Changes in Consumption Patterns across Generations

Foreword

Historically, old age and consumption have rarely addressed each other directly. Housed in different disciplines, they have been associated with opposite social agendas and views of life. Ageing emerged as a subject of social gerontology and social medicine with a focus on illness, poverty, dependence, and death. By contrast, consumer culture, especially since the 1950s, has sparked debates about affluence, shopping, choice and a hedonistic lifestyle. Consumption here appeared youthful, fashionable, and sexy—a rebellion against "old society," its hierarchies, and values. In the last decade, this simple divide has been successfully challenged and crossed from a number of directions. Older people are not just patients or poor: they are consumers, too. Their lifestyles, it is increasingly recognized, have major consequences for social policy and sustainability as well as for the economy and their own well-being. And, old people were once young too, which leads to the important question about how material lifestyles are carried over into old age. Research on consumption, meanwhile, has slowly shaken off its association with shopping, choice, and conspicuous consumption. It involves daily routines and ordinary practices like gardening, eating, or pursuing a hobby, as well as shopping. And, far from just being driven by selfish individualism or attempts to keep up with the Jones', consumers have been found to care about their families, community, and distant others. There are, thus, a growing number of synergies and points of contact between research on ageing and research on consumption that make for interesting cross-fertilization between these fields. To foster such exchange was one of the aims of the Cultures of Consumption Research Programme (2002-07). This book is one of the results (www.consume.bbk.ac.uk). It offers readers a guide through the changing landscape of ageing and consumption, pointing to new theories, questions, and policy implications.

There are good reasons why older people have moved to the forefront of public and commercial attention. Some of these concern absolute changes, some relative or qualitative ones. The proportion of old people in the population as a whole has almost doubled in so-called developed societies in the last century. Some of this is an optical illusion—the share of older people naturally went up as the number of children who died young radically declined. The old have always been with us: in Arezzo in 1427 Italy, 16 percent of citizens were sixty or older. In recent years, the much talked about "ageing" of Europe, is in part "de-younging." A society like Italy, for example, looks older not because there are many more people aged 65 to 74 about, but rather because the number of 15- to 24-year-olds has dropped sharply from 900,000 to under 600,000 in the last 15 years.

Still, even with such qualifications, the position of the elderly has changed in a number of profound ways in the course of the last century. By the 1970s, 25 to 30 percent of people over 25 years old were 60+ in OCED countries (in the late nineteenth century it was around 15 to 20 percent). In the same time period, the labor force participation of men 65 and over declined from between 66 to 75 percent, to today's 10 to 20 percent. Above all, older people are richer and fitter today than they were 30 or 40 years ago. People over 65 are no longer worse off than other age groups. Poverty has not been eliminated, but the number of old people living below the poverty line has shrunk dramatically since the 1970s. Old people own property, assets, and holiday homes. Indeed, older people in Japan and Germany spend more on recreation and culture than their younger cohorts. That policy makers and media are talking about "active ageing" should come as little as a surprise as the commercial interest in the "grey market."

What will be more surprising, is that today's debate about the consumption and leisure patterns of consumers is not the first one to confront these developments. The baby-boom generation that grew up after the Second World War in a context of affluence, commercial youth culture, full employment, and (for most) no military service is currently at the center of inquiry. It takes "the Sixties" as its starting point and asks about the generational effects of the "consumerism" associated with that decade on baby boomers as they are entering old age today. But debates about "successful ageing" and the contribution of leisure reach back in time at least to the 1930s and 1940s. In the United States, this was a debate shaped, in part, by the challenge of retirement for self-esteem, status, inclusion, and the organization of everyday life. How would a group of retired consumers fit into a society of laborers? Hannah Arendt expressed this dilemma sharply in *The Human Condition* in 1959: "What we are confronted with is the prospect of a society of laborers without labor, that is, without the only activity left to them. Surely, nothing could be worse" (p.5). Loss of a position could mean loss of recognition and the beginning of exclusion and disengagement from civic life more generally. Could the lawyer or accountant count on the same recognition in his local Rotary Club after retirement? Might old people be lost in a deluge of free time and end up in front of the TV? The parallel increase in longevity and leisure time could, thus, appear as an early harbinger of civic decline and an erosion of associational ties.

But the discovery of leisure and older consumers also drew on positive ideals of "active ageing." One came straight out of the experience of the Second World War and the depression that preceded it. Older people themselves were becoming more active, mobile, and leisure oriented in the inter-war years, trying to create new communities, to keep themselves fit, and to fight loneliness. Early trailer-park retirement communities were springing up in the 1930s. One of their appeals was shared recreational activities and mutual respect amongst the retired. By 1950 already, over one-quarter of Florida's old people had moved there. The over 60s took out a disproportionate share of passports to travel. The expansion of leisure amongst the elderly in these years shows how Arendt's "society of laborers" was already in a state of transformation—with values, identities, and social mechanisms shifting from production to consumption. A silent revolution was under way—of shuffleboards, bingo, choir, and Saturday night dances that was no less important than the showy, vocal transformation of commercial youth culture associated with the "Sixties."

It is, therefore, debatable whether we should think in terms of a neat succession of work society followed by consumer society. The image and self-understanding of elderly people in the 1940s-50s was already more positive and dynamic than the picture of a work-obsessed society would make one expect. "These are the best years of my life," so enjoyable, "that I almost wish it could go on forever" was a common response that Havinghurst and Albrecht had when they interviewed older Americans immediately after the Second World War (*Older People*, New York, 1953: 48ff.). Many older people understood that staying active enhanced social, physical, and psychological well-being. When Havinghurst and others developed the theory of "successful ageing" (1963), they were in part drawing on observable changes in the elderly population itself.

How should we evaluate the switch from "welfare dependents" to "active consumers" that has marked public policy and discourse in the last few decades? Some recent scholars have rightly pointed to the negative side effects of the currently dominant discourse of "active ageing" in advertising and social policy. Declining physical strength, ailments, and the end of life remain part of ageing. To be surrounded by images of eternal youth does put psychological pressure on people with ageing bodies. A 2001 study by the AARP found that half the baby boomers in the United States are depressed about getting old, with one in ten contemplating cosmetic surgery. At the same time, research with elderly people and their activities shows how a rise in activity levels (from card games to competitive athletics) has increased well-being and social participation. In addition to discursive critiques of "active ageing," the practices and voices of older people themselves deserve to be heard more often. Older people have played an active role in the evolution of "active ageing."

One step forward, developed in this volume, is to think of the "third age" less in terms of a shared life stage with identifiable characteristics, and more as a cultural field that different age groups can more or less associate with. The wholesale label "old" or "elderly" is, of course, only of limited use. Age is in the eye of the beholder; well into the nineteenth century, it was not uncommon for women in parts of Europe to be seen to enter old age when they turned thirty. But it also depends on a range of unevenly distributed socio-economic and cultural resources—and on sheer genetic luck. Read alongside each other, the chapters in this volume document the on-going diversity of what old age means within the context of shared overall changes. The growing number of cars, VCRs, telephones, and computers in elderly people's homes shows growing convergence with the rest of the population. At the same time, education, income, and living arrangements remain diverse. So do people's self-perception of their bodies and generational identities. Put together, the result is a considerable diversity of ageing consumer lifestyles, as several chapters show.

Diversity extends to the place where people do most of the consuming: the home. Elderly people in affluent societies today have radically different living arrangements. In Europe and the United States, elderly people now mostly live alone. In the United Kingdom, only 15 percent of old people live in households with younger members, compared to two-thirds a century earlier. Meanwhile, in Italy and many Asian societies, living with children remains the norm for many elderly people. It would be fallacious to postulate here some clash between consuming cultures—one individualist, the other collective. The rise of solo living has not meant the end of the family—baby boomers value family time, and caring between the young and the old continues, simply through more flexible, less intimate living arrangements. As most elderly spend more time at home than outside the home, such drastic differences, however, have enormous repercussions for everyday consumption routines, in all their social, cultural, and environmental dimensions.

Attention to the diversity of ageing makes a significant contribution to our more general understanding of the logics of consumption in contemporary societies. Contrary to the popular image of Americanization and convergence, affluent societies continue to diverge in the way people live and spend their time and money. The focus on generations advocated in this volume holds the promise of telling us more about how such patterns of consumption emerge and are carried forward across time, and about the generationally specific factors that favor certain predispositions and habits over others. There has been seminal work on the importance of generation for children growing up during the depression years in the United States. Deprivation, unemployment, and uncertainty in the early 1930s shaped attitudes towards money and led to a more family and leisure-oriented lifestyle when this cohort reached adulthood after the Second World War. This volume takes the discussion of generations one step further, exploring the ways in which "the miracle years" of growth and affluence in the 1950s-60s affected the generational habitus of baby boomers. That baby boomers are taking with them into old age a more cosmopolitan, mobile, and travel-oriented lifestyle, is just one finding. The chapters that follow show how the interweaving of generation and consumption can provide fresh insights for students of old age and consumer culture alike.

—Professor Frank Trentmann
London, May 2008

Preface

The chapters in this volume are based on research papers given at an international workshop on generation and consumption held in London in February 2007. They provide a unique collective contribution, from a diversity of perspectives, to the debates surrounding generational change in contemporary consumer societies.

The book addresses the rise of consumer culture and the various attempts to explain and account for it. Specifically, the book considers the view that a particular generational entelechy formed in the post-war period and this has been carried on into the early twentieth century with particular consequences for the experience of later life. The rise of individualism, of mass consumption, leisure, and lifestyle have been accompanied by the democratization of social forms and for many a corrosion of community and social cohesion. Each chapter in the book offers a unique perspective on the complexity of these social changes highlighting how understanding is gained from examining the generational habitus that developed in tandem with the rise of mass consumption in the post-war period.

The book begins by examining how advances in social theory have responded to the rise of consumer society and how consumer lifestyles have become increasingly salient to the understanding of social structure and conflict in later modern societies. Drawing on historical perspectives and comparative studies, the book then addresses arguments surrounding the conceptualization of social change with reference to generational effects and generational conflict. While recognizing the strengths and weaknesses of adopting a generational approach to social change, the book develops an argument that emphasizes the importance of generational effects for the understanding of later life. Having set the scene in terms of the literature on consumption, lifestyles, and generational change, key questions are raised in relation to the transformation of later life that are addressed in turn by the contributors to this volume.

1

Consumption and Generational Change: The Rise of Consumer Lifestyles

Ian Rees Jones, Paul Higgs, and David J. Ekerdt

All that is solid melts into air.
—Marx and Engels

I hope I die before I grow old
—The Who

Introduction

Many have chosen to revisit Marx and Engels' famous metaphor of the rapidity of change in the capitalism of their day and point to its prescience for contemporary social relations. The complex solidities of the old order that anchored social science over decades have become more confusing and more in need of revision. Nowhere can this be said to be truer than in relation to the expansion of the field of consumption in social life. Moving from being a relatively unimportant part of the processes of production, distribution, and exchange, how people consume and to what ends has moved to centre stage. In many ways this shift echoes and continues the concerns outlined by Marx and Engels. For them, a key feature of the social transformations that they were commenting on was the international reach of industrial capitalism and its push to open new markets across the globe and in so doing giving rise to new wants and desires. The cosmopolitan capitalism of twenty-first-century society is one exemplified by a truly global arena of consumption in which distance is no obstacle to the distribution and ownership of

1

a large range of consumer products. Equally, the social and cultural distinctions that accompanied more classically "modern" forms of consumption have been subjected to the same kind of flattening that has been experienced in relation to "high" and "popular" culture. The contemporary experience of consumption has eroded some of the associations between rank and privilege that participation and ownership of some consumption practices and commodities previously buttressed. At the same time the growing focus on distinctiveness and individual difference, which emerges out of growing consumer markets, allows for both the transgression and re-articulation of continually changing boundaries within consumption practices. Avant gardes rise, become popular with greater numbers, fall from fashion and are finally "ironically" re-incorporated as retro or are integrated into a new fusion. In this process of flux, are situated the collective and individual life histories of the generations who created and lived through these changes. These generational experiences of consumption are both fixed by period and transformed by age.

Some of the largest beneficiaries of this expansion of consumerism are members of the same generation as Roger Daltrey who, when singing of the desire to die before becoming old, epitomized the cult of youth that saturated the culture both of the sixties and subsequent decades. George Orwell once noted that "each generation imagines itself to be more intelligent than the one that went before it, and wiser than the one that comes after it." and the post-war "boomer" generation was no different in this respect. Its members made great play of drawing distinctions between their own actions and the staid, sober, and conservative habits of preceding generations. As memories of inter-war economic depression receded and rationing gave way to economic growth and the rise of the affluent society, teenage consumers became symbols of the cultural zeitgeist even if their sub-cultures were of little relevance to the experiences of the rest of the population (Sandbrook, 2005; 2006; Marwick, 2003). But there was more to this than the tendencies toward inter-generational fracture over the life course. In contrast to preceding generations, the life course of the post-war generation coincided with a period in history that led to the consolidation of mass consumption and consumer society.

In bringing together the twin themes of consumption and generational change we are aware that there is a strong, we would say productive, tension between those working within a sociological framework who tend to see discontinuities in the rise of new forms of consumption in the post-war era and those working within a historical framework who see patterns of continuity in consumption over longer periods (Trentmann, 2004). Whilst recognizing that each generational group may, in general, experience many phenomena that appear to be "new" to them but in fact have a longer pedigree when viewed through a historical lens, there are key aspects to the periodization and experiences of the post-war generational group that separate it out from other cohorts. First, they were born following the trauma of a world war and expectations for the construction of a better society in the aftermath of that war were high and located in that generational group. Second, as they progressed through their own life courses, the life course in general became de-institutionalized. And, in effect, they were neophytes who contributed to that de-institutionalization often by trying to find rational responses to changing circumstances. Third, they grew up in a period of affluence and growth, and participated in the labor market during cycles of rapid growth and recession not depression. Fourth, they entered adulthood at a time of political and social upheaval where new ideas, new forms of citizenship, individual freedoms, and legal rights were coming together. They participated in and helped form the growth of new social movements during this period. Campaigning social movements may have a longer pedigree than post-war libertarian movements and, while not all social movements endure (Tilly, 2004), the interaction of these new social movements with existing institutions gave these movements and their participants a profound sense of being instigators of change (Tilly and Tarrow, 2007). Finally, they constructed and became engaged with emerging new technologies that created radical changes to contraception, communication, work, travel, and living conditions—all of which opened up new opportunities for practices of consumption and leisure. These changes, it is argued, provided the context for the development of a generational habitus that was radically different to those of previous generations—a generational habitus that the post-war generations helped forge and reproduce, and carry with them into later life.

These changes have led many to write of a crisis of ageing as these generations experience longevity and appear to be entering later life fully engaged with consumerism. As Blackburn (2002) points out, the longevity revolution is too easily presented as either a dystopian crisis or a wonderful utopia of health, wealth, and vitality in later life. It is important to note that the contemporary dynamics of global capitalism in tandem with forms of neo-liberal politics provide a framework that leads to relatively high rates of investment in sites of consumption, shopping malls, and financial property with comparable disinvestment in public spaces and public provision. Indeed, the financial arrangements around retirement have been at the center of this re-commodification with much of inflow of funds to global stock markets being fuelled by the pension funds of many low and middle-income groups. The "hollowing out" of the welfare state in relation to the provision of social/state pension funds has also been backed up by the putative specters of generational conflict emerging from the promotion of an extended youth culture by "selfish" baby boomers who wish to have it all.

The chapters in this volume are based on papers given at an international workshop on generation and consumption held in London in February of 2007. They provide a collective contribution, from a diversity of perspectives, to the debates surrounding generational change in contemporary consumer societies. Forming a framework for the discussion, we address the rise of consumer culture and the various attempts to explain and account for it. We then consider arguments for the view that a particular generational entelechy formed in the post-war period and this has been carried on into the early twentieth century with particular consequences for the experience of later life. The rise of individualism, of mass consumption, leisure, and lifestyles have been accompanied by the democratization of social forms and for many a corrosion of community and social cohesion (Sennett, 2006). We argue that an understanding of the complexity of these social changes is gained from examining the generational habitus that developed in tandem with the rise of mass consumption in the post-war period. To develop the argument, we first consider how social theory has responded to the rise of consumer society and how consumer lifestyles have become increasingly salient to the understanding of social structure and conflict in later modern societies. We then address arguments surrounding the conceptualization of social change with reference to generational effects and generational conflict. While recognizing the strengths and weaknesses of adopting a generational approach to social change we highlight the importance of generational effects for the understanding of later life. Having set the scene in terms of the literature on consumption, lifestyles, and generational change we then raise some key questions in relation to the transformation of later life that are addressed in turn by the contributors to this volume.

Consumer Culture and the Rise of Lifestyle Identities

Lifestyle has become a key motif for chroniclers of social and cultural change over the last half century. The boom in lifestyle media and the rise of cultural intermediaries has been linked by a number of social and cultural theorists to the rise of postmodern culture (Bell and Hollows, 2006). The concept of lifestyles is, however, not a recent one. Weber defined lifestyles as forms of behavior realized by choices made within the limits of social context or structures (Weber, 1987 [1922]). That is, lifestyles constructed forms of distinction that identified particular status groups. These ideas can be seen in the work of Veblen (1931 [1899]) who, in particular, pointed out the gendered nature of conspicuous consumption among the rising middle classes of America at the end of the nineteenth century. Consumption, as a means of signifying status, was mostly seen in pejorative terms by Veblen. These ideas were taken further by Simmel (2004) who argued that modern life was increasingly objectified and commodified thus leading to more troubling relationships between the subjective and objective worlds. Forms of consumption and taste became important markers of status in social interaction. These trends were closely related in Simmel's thought to forces at work in the modern city whose inhabitants, being hyper-stimulated, developed a blasé mentality. Money became valued for itself rather than just a means of exchange, and imitation of the consumption habits and fashions of the upper class became an important means of signifying social mobility. As Tim Edwards argues (Edwards, 2000) the dark side to consumer society has been a key feature of the sociological and historical literature for some time. Marxist writers have tended to see consumption trends as epiphenomena or the result of false consciousness among passive workers who are duped into new wants and desires. The dark side of consumption is also evident in Benjamin's (1973) work on the city where the Flaneur epitomises the self regarding, empty headed, shallow consumer engaged in a fruitless search for satisfaction. Even the post-modernist leaning Bauman is critical of the "pernicious impact" of consumer society which he sees as leading to, among other things, "social deskilling" (Bauman and Tester, 2001).

While earlier writers tried to address consumption among elites and the rise of modernity in terms of alienation, forms of consciousness, and psychosocial struggle more recent writers have addressed consumption in the context of mass consumerism. In the post-war era as consumption began to saturate the social field, starting in the USA but spreading rapidly to western Europe, it gave rise to opportunities for emulation of particular forms of taste and style thus leading to a democratization of consumption practices and a need for forms of distinction to be continually reinvented to keep ahead of emulative and adaptive processes (Corrigan, 1997). These new concerns can be found in Bourdieu's work on forms of distinction in French society (Bourdieu, 1984). Although Bourdieu has been criticized for fixing working-class culture to allow him to present a case for forms of cultural capital being granted legitimation through relations of power,[1] his contribution is of vital importance because, in France at least, he identified the rise of the new middle class and new legitimate cultural forms that replaced old notions of conformity, sobriety, and classicism with more hedonistic approaches based around consuming and shopping focused, in particular, on the domestic sphere.

Again, these ideas were taken further by those who interpreted the rise of consumer lifestyles in the late twentieth century as marking an important rupture with the austere and conformist post-war period (Featherstone, 1991). Other sociologists have followed this lead to argue that the shift away from productivism to consumerism has been accompanied by a greater concern with the construction of identities and distinctions through consumption and the choice of lifestyles (Bauman, 1998; Giddens, 1991). In late modern consumer societies, lifestyles have become increasingly important as signifiers of status and identity. The emphasis on the multiplicity of choices available to individuals, from which identities are constructed, is one of the pillars of these approaches (Warde, 2002). Consumption itself, it is argued, has been transformed away from one with a direct link to mass production to a flexible specialized post-Fordist form of consumption where distinction is based on capturing personal forms of style in niche markets (Edwards, 2000). Practices of consumption are played out and continually re-worked in the media and Giddens (1991) has argued that lifestyle media provide a guide to living within late modernity. Where individuals are caught up in the anxieties of being free to choose with the responsibility of having to choose wisely (Bauman, 1998) such guidance may be a way of offering a sense of ontological security in a world where choices become multiplied and the judging between competing forms of culture and taste becomes more difficult for individuals to negotiate. As Barry Schwartz points out, there is some evidence to suggest that an excess of choice can have a damaging and corrosive effect on individual well-being as well as social relations (Schwartz, et al., 2002). Also as Daniel Horowitz argues, whilst there have been massive gains for Western populations in terms of escape from the grinding poverty of the early decades of the twentieth century, these have been accompanied by new forms of anxiety, insecurity, and social troubles (Horowitz, 2004). This has led some to strike a moralistic tone highlighting the selfish, materialistic, and corrupting aspects of consumerism and focusing on a perceived decline in mechanisms of social control, deferred gratification and thrift, and the rise of short-term and hedonistic attitudes (Offer, 2006). A claim for declining social cohesion in the United States over the last fifty years has been made by Putnam (2001) who argues that this decline springs from a generational break between the values of the generation that fought in the Second World War and the values of subsequent generations. It is to this perceived generational fracture and its forms that we now turn.

A Post-War Generational Entelechy?

References to generational change and generational conflict are likely to stimulate sharp division within social science. On the one hand are those who see in the concept of generation a salience that can help unpick the social changes, particularly cultural changes of the last few decades (Gilleard and Higgs, 2005). Others, however, find the term too vague and ephemeral for any form of operationalization to be possible (Ryder, 1965). The idea that one of the key drivers of social change has been the particular mentality of a generational group or a generational entelechy has been around for some time (Mannheim 1952, 1997). Mannheim was particularly concerned with the capacity of a generational unit or group to drive social transformations rather than simply the reproduction of social life. The problem, as Mannheim himself noted, was how one could study such ephemeral phenomena as generational entelechy. At a methodological level there is a continuous tension between the concepts of age, cohort, period, and generation that has not yet been adequately resolved. It is perhaps just these methodological problems that have constrained attempts to take Mannheim's work forward. However, more recently Bryan Turner has suggested that as dynamics of class relations and class stratification change, it may be that generational takes on new salience in the study of social change (Turner, 1998). Just as Mannheim related ruptures between generational groups to the catastrophe of the First World War, Edmunds and Turner (2002) suggest that traumatic events, such as responses to the Vietnam War, have been key to the formation of generational conflict, generational divides, and the birth of new forms of generational consciousness in the late twentieth century and early twenty-first century (Turner, 2002).

The argument presented here is that while there are strong continuities in terms of forms of power, particularly modes of production, coercion, and persuasion (Runciman, 1997) post-war transformations have been profound in the fields of lifestyles, consumption, and status identity. These transformations have been experienced and driven by key generational groups and crucially have not been shed by subsequent generational groups. It is ironic that the economic foundations constructed by the post-war welfare consensus gave rise to a generational habitus framed around the valorization of choice, individualism, a distrust of state institutions, and a democratization of culture. This generational habitus is reproduced in later life as an increasing proportion of people have the resources available to them in old age to continue to pursue consumer lifestyles. Instead of the "improving culture" that Laslett (1996 [1989]) envisaged as part of the duties of the third age, there are more varied and fragmented cultural forms. Of course, many will choose traditional paths of leisure, activity, and voluntarism in the third age, but equally many others will choose alternative perhaps more hedonistic lifestyle forms. One of the important sociological questions that needs to be addressed in relation to these changes is the extent to which these choices are made deliberately and reflexively concomitant with the rise of the quasi subject in late modernity (Beck, Bonss, and Lau, 2003).

Our argument is that the ways in which these generational identities are embedded in current social phenomena have not been adequately addressed. There is a need to consider the extent to which generational forces and consumer identities are influencing the forms of social relations in areas such as new religious movements, new household forms, social conflict, and class, race, and gender relations. There is also a need to undertake more comparative work to examine the extent to which generational effects of social change operate in different historical, political, economic, and cultural settings.

Perspectives on Consumption and Generation

The chapters in this volume draw on detailed empirical work to address key questions that arise from the interplay between the rise of mass consumption, increasing individualization, and generational fracture. These include, what role does consumerism play in the changing nature of religion in the twenty-first century?

Are there key transformations in attitudes towards ageing, death, and spirituality that are generationally driven? In what ways are materialistic values reproduced generationally, and how do these values determine patterns of inter-generational transfers and the disposal of consumer objects? Should we see the rise and spread of global consumer culture as simply the expansion of American culture, or is there a more complex and multivalent process at work? Just as early writers on consumption highlighted forms of class distinction associated with consumption practices, are there modes of consumption and distinction discernible between generational groups? Have there been shifts in the experience of later life that are strongly associated with particular generational groups? If so, does this mean that we can no longer refer to the old or elderly as a social category? Are there historical continuities in both practices of consumption and the lived reality of old age that are being ignored in the rush to mark and epochal shift to late modernity?

The literature on consumption and consumer society is replete with abstract theoretical debates about the symbolic value of consumer goods and the impact of hyper-commodification on the human condition; but what evidence do we have to support the view that consumption and consumerism are dominating social lives? Has consumption saturated the social field or are there groups, particularly generational cohorts, that have either been excluded or lag behind others? To what extent can we talk of "The baby boomer" as a homogenous group that has driven these changes? Do people that were part of the baby boomer cohorts have a boomer identity? Are there differences in these generational effects between different countries, or is this essentially an American phenomenon? To what extent is the American experience driving these changes on a global scale, and to what extent are there cultural differences in consumption and generational change in Europe, Asia, Africa, and across the developing world? In order to address some of these questions we have divided the volume into three sections: Theoretical Perspectives on Generations and Consumption, Historical Dimensions of Generation and Consumption, and International Comparisons of Changes in Consumption Patterns across Generations.

Theoretical Perspectives on Generations and Consumption

In Chapter 2, entitled The Third Age: Field, Habitus, or Identity?, Chris Gilleard and Paul Higgs suggest that the idea of distinctions between generational groups is key to understanding the third age as a cultural field in which actors from various cohorts and life stages participate. As an alternative to Peter Laslett's original description of the third age as a "new" stage of life, they suggest, instead, that the third age is viewed as a cultural field with which some members of "late-life" cohorts are more deeply engaged than others. Such a perspective draws parallels between Mannheim's concept of a generational unit and its accompanying generational style and Bourdieu's concept of a cultural field and its accompanying habitus. They focus on two important aspects to this. First, there is the possibility of generational fracture in consumption practices; and second, there may be a more general shift from consuming things to consuming experiences (including religious experiences). The capacity to consume particular experiences thus becomes a key signifier of social stratification in the future. Consumerism provides an underlying logic to the formation of the third age and the lifestyles that shape and are shaped by it. In defending their generational approach, they argue that while cohort analysis is a useful tool to explore hypotheses about the nature and boundaries of the third age, it is important to avoid conferring on such tools an explanatory power they cannot bear.

In Chapter 3, entitled Goods Not Gods: New Spiritualities, Consumerism, and Religious Markets, Bryan S. Turner notes that despite, or even because of, the large body of work addressing the relationship between religion and production there is very little work addressing religion and consumption. This is surprising given the rapid growth of religious consumerism in recent decades. At the same time, there are strong connections between generational change, the blurring of ageing, death and bodily boundaries, and the growth of religiosity in the form of prosperity cults. Furthermore, the interrelationship between the growth in consumption and changes to the power of religious organizations is driving the democratization of religion. The delayed gratification and reward in heaven of pious religions does not work in a post-scarcity world were heaven on earth is available now. In the US, for example, Christianity has renounced its original theology of death and redemption from sin and adjusted to the imperatives of consumer society so that, like early religions that were prosperity cults, churches offer material rewards to members. Turner draws connections between these religious transformations and the experiences of post-war generational groups—particularly the baby boomer generations in the context of growing affluence. It is, he argues, through examining the impact of baby boomers on religious practices and consciousness that we will understand religious consciousness in the USA. A large post-war generation, through their engagement in consumer culture, is redrawing the boundaries of mainstream popular religion. Furthermore, in a consumer culture the traditional moral authority of religion declines in the face of commercial prosperity cults based around wealth and health. He concludes that we are witnessing the growth of religious markets offering religious lifestyles as consumption so that in late or second modernity "Gods can be goods."

As generations age, there are also interesting questions relating to the turning away from material things. As David Ekerdt outlines in "Dispossession: The Tenacity of Things," the extent to which there is a generational aspect to the concept of dis-consumption has not been fully developed. Our possession of things reflects consumption practices according to age, period, and cohort influences—and there may be generational differences in possession/dispossession propensities. The bonds between us and the things we possess help form identities; but, as Ekerdt argues, capitalism has the capacity to commodify anything including practices of dispossession. This can be witnessed in the increasing market for dis-consumption methods such as "de-cluttering." He also describes poignantly the dilemmas, anxieties, and frustrations that arise from the weight of possession. These dilemmas weigh heavily on individuals regardless of their income, status, or the value of the things they possess. The under researched area of gifting and inter-generational transfers is an important aspect of this. Much of the moral panic surrounding the ageing of the baby boomers is focused on their materialistic values that are predicted to clash with the growing gap in the burden of care and caring. By focusing on dis-consumption, Ekerdt highlights the limits to such simplistic accounts.

Historical Dimensions of Generation and Consumption

Pat Thane, in Old Age, Consumption, and Change over Time (Chapter 5), draws on a range of historical sources to suggest that the changing consumption patterns of older people over the past century mirror those of younger people. This is because older people today have higher incomes, better health, and more time for leisure, while many items of consumption have become relatively less expensive. However, Thane argues that we should be wary of stereotyping older people at any time in the past as less active, more passive, consumers than younger people. Her discussion of representations of older people in history suggests that the recognition of the heterogeneity of ageing has a long pedigree. Thane reminds us that older people participated in the expansion in availability of consumer goods in the eighteenth century, but historians are hampered by a lack of data, particularly on middle class consumption patterns. Nevertheless, it was not until the period following the Second World War that retirement developed into a phase of relative leisure and relaxation sitting between a period of employment and decrepitude/death. She suggests that this transformation was gendered and more traumatic for men who were less likely than women to have developed social networks outside of work. Drawing on Townsend's UK study of East Enders in London in the 1950s, she highlights how retirement for working-class men was associated with a loss of status, dependency, shame, and financial curtailment in consumption patterns. In the 1980s and 1990s, retirement spread to younger age groups. Post-war retirement generally benefited from broader secular increases in affluence so that previous associations of old age with poverty began to be re-placed by an old age that reflected the class, gender, and ethnic divisions of wider society. While older people have increased in both number and heterogeneity, the cultural understandings of old age have changed making attempts to define them as a group increasingly anachronistic. Furthermore, differences among older people continue to be as stark as those between them and people of other age groups.

In Ageing, Cohorts, and Consumption: The British Experience 1968-2005 (Chapter 6) Martin Hyde and colleagues give flesh to these historical insights by charting the ownership of key consumer goods and expenditure on key items by retired households since the 1960s. They ask whether baby boomers are driving a new, consumerist experience of later life or did the 1960s' generation create a new generational habitus that has spread out, albeit unevenly, to encompass other age groups radically transforming later life for all? They identify two closely related theories for the rise in consumer lifestyles amongst older people today. The *cohort hypothesis* states that the demographic weight of the "baby-boomers" created the necessary conditions for a mass-consumer society and that this cohort is the vanguard of this consumer culture. In contrast, the *generational hypothesis* states that changes in the organization of capitalism during the 1960s created a consumer society which, despite its initial emergence amongst youth culture, has colonized all age strata. Furthermore, this transformation of later life would have occurred with or without the baby boom. By undertaking a pseudo-cohort analysis of a series of expenditure surveys for the UK between 1968 and 2005, they chart the patterns of expenditure and ownership of goods amongst British retirees and explore the relationships between ageing, cohort, and consumption within this context. Their findings show that, in the UK, retirees became increasingly engaged in consumption through the purchase of household goods and similar in their patterns of expenditure to other age groups. They propose that the lack of any age-associated decline in ownership of most goods suggests that this phenomenon is generalized and not simply restricted to the baby boomers. This is further supported by the general trend towards convergence in rates of ownership of items like telephones and TVs. In fact, a large part of this convergence in established goods is due to the baby boomers catching up with the already relatively high rates of ownership in other cohorts. Inter-cohort differences in expenditure are evident with older cohorts seeming to spend slightly higher proportions on basic categories, such as food and fuel, than those in the younger cohorts. In turn, there is some evidence to support the argument that baby boomers spend more on luxury or leisure goods such as household goods. Thus, when one looks at ownership of established goods and, to some extent, expenditure the evidence appears to support the generational hypothesis, while the data on novel goods appear to support the cohort hypothesis.

International Comparisons of Changes in Consumption Patterns across Generations

In Chapter 7, entitled Housing Crisis, Generational Inequalities, and Welfare States, Fanny Bugeja presents a timely reminder that secular and generational changes may be accompanied by changes in the nature and patterning of inequalities. By undertaking an analysis of UK and French housing expenditure data between 1985 and 2000, Bugeja identifies differences in house purchasing, financial forms, patterns and rules, systems of housing benefits, and the patterning of tenure. Her analysis leads her to argue that the UK appears to have low intergenerational inequalities in terms of property, while France has high intergenerational inequalities. France also seems to have high intergenerational inequalities in terms of housing expenditure, whilst in the UK inequalities seem more closely related to labor-market status. Moreover, housing expenditure inequalities appeared to fall relatively faster in the UK in the last decades of the twentieth century. Bugeja concludes that French society has experienced a comparative increase in both intergenerational and intra-generational inequality, while in the UK the welfare regime seem to have contributed to reducing intergenerational wealth inequalities.

The US experience is addressed in detail by George Moschis in Chapter 8, entitled Generational Marketing, which traces the evolution of the mature market in the US. Here there is evidence both of differences in the consumption patterns of generational groups and the gradually awakening of corporate America to the consumer power of older generations. Moschis divides the evolution of generational marketing (targeting of age cohorts) into three phases: neglect, raised awareness, and increasing sophistication. Sophistication and refinement is seen in increasing segmentation of generational markets and increasing age segmentation of specific products (for example, insurance services). Despite this, Moschis feels the need to develop guidelines for companies who still appear to find generational factors difficult to address. With respect to the US baby boomer generations, Moschis outlines the values and lifestyles of these generational groups that are related to their consumer behavior. He emphasizes instant gratification, indulgence, youthfulness, and nostalgia. Characterized as being "health conscious, time poor and stressed" their concerns translate into new forms and patterns of consumption; combing risk aversion and propensity to save with luxury spending, and credit-based shopping. Much generational marketing appears to focus on selling products that are likely to address what older people want and need by avoiding any associations with old age. But this is double edged—for, as Moschis argues, a product or shopping space that becomes recognised as being mature is swiftly rejected precisely because its success in addressing these wants and needs engenders connotations with old age.

Finally in Chapter 9, Comparing Welfare Regime Changes: Living Standards and the Unequal Life Chances of Different Birth Cohorts, Louis Chauvel draws on comparative data to highlight the extent to which different welfare regimes face severe generational inequalities, the consequences of which could be the long-term destabilization of some contemporary welfare systems. Chauvel focuses on inter- and intra-cohort inequalities in living standards. He highlights the emergence of "scarring effects" that influence specific birth cohorts in countries where the welfare regime engenders an increasing polarization between middle-aged insiders and young outsiders. To illustrate his arguments, Chauvel considers four types of welfare regimes: France as an exemplar of a corporatist (or conservative), the US as an example of a liberal regime, Denmark as an example of a universalist (or social democratic) regime, Italy as an example of a familialistic regime. After outlining a framework for generational analysis, he presents a series of analyses showing trends in occupational mobility, the distribution of income, and intra-cohort inequality between these different countries. Chauvel argues that in France and Italy, today's seniors benefit from a large welfare state, but younger generations may not be able to benefit in the same way from the rights and entitlements won by previous generational groups. He goes further to suggest that this places huge pressures on these welfare regimes. The problem, however, is not stagnation but lack of preparation in the long term at the expense of younger generations. In contrast, in the US inequalities are based on class, gender, status, and race rather than generational differences. Younger generations in high income and status groups enjoy exceptionally better positions, while the middle class see their incomes stagnate and the poor suffer significant material deprivation. Up until the banking crisis of 2008, this regime has appeared stable but has high levels of inequality. The Danish system is based on high standards of protection, equality, and solidarity and appears inter-generationally stable since newer cohorts benefit from similar conditions and rights as their elders. In terms of consumption, these findings give some insight into differences in standards of living over the life course in these different regime types. For example, in France compared to the US, it would appear that younger generational groups face real difficulties, while seniors benefit disproportionally from the welfare system and economic growth. In Italy, the youth face similar problems as in France, but a greater degree of familialistic dependence reduces the immediate visibility of the social problem. Finally, Denmark seems to be a stable model of a universalistic solidaristic regime. The emphasis on equality results in a smoothing of differences in income and expenditure. While recognizing there are limitations to the welfare regime model approach, this analysis suggests the universalistic welfare regime is sustainable and maintains its own capacity for long-term development. By contrasting "generational fracture" across these different welfare regimes, we are reminded that generational change may follow different trajectories in different parts of the world.

Conclusion

We began this discussion with a reference to the obsession of post-war culture with youth and the concomitant rejection of older generations. While there are strong continuities in terms of forms of power, post-war transformations have been profound in the fields of lifestyles, consumption, and status identity. These transformations have been experienced and driven by key generational groups who are taking these attitudes and values with them into later life. We would suggest that there is a tendency in the sociological literature to view these changes, particularly to later life, in apocalyptic language. While not underestimating the rise in global inequality and the negative consequences of run-away consumerism, it is important to remember the positive potential of recent social transformations. For example, rather than viewing global networks as prompting new forms of surveillance and control, it is possible that people are finding their own way in the new networked public sphere—in ways that can threaten forms of autocracy and domination (Eder, 2003). As others before us have pointed out (Bell, 1973; Slater, 1999) consumer culture developed from market societies and commercialization. As such, it has become a universal phenomenon that constructs unlimited wants and desires, promotes individualism, and provides the framework for the construction of new and multiple identities. Within second modernity, it is an important mechanism for the exercise of power and inequality. The chapters that follow utilize detailed empirical work to consider the extent to which generational forces and consumer identities are influencing new forms of social relations and changing the face of later life in the early twenty-first century.

Note

1.   When upper-class individuals are seen to engage in forms of working-class culture, in Bourdieu's world they are seen to do so with a sense of ironic distance. The working class, on the other hand, are considered incapable of such an intellectual approach to their cultural forms (Bennet, 2006).

References

Bauman, Z. (1998). *Work, Consumerism and the New Poor.* Buckingham: Open University Press.

Bauman, Z. and Tester, K. (2001). *Conversations with Zygmunt Bauman.* Cambridge: Polity.

Bell, D. (1973). *The Coming of Post-Industrial Society.* New York: Basic Books.

Bell, D. & Hollows, J. (2006). *Historicizing Lifestyle, Mediating Taste, Consumption and Identity from the 1900s to 1970s.* Aldershot: Ashgate.

Benjamin, W. (1973). *Illuminations*. London: Fontana.

Bennet, T. (2006). "Aesthetics and social ordering in the work of Pierre Bourdieu: a critique." Paper presented at ISA World Conference of Sociology, Durban.

Blackburn, R. (2002). *Banking on Death or Investing in Life: The History and Future of Pensions*. London: Verso.

Bourdieu, P. (1984). *Distinction: A Social Critique of Judgement and Taste*. Cambridge, MA: Harvard University Press.

Corrigan, P (1997). *The Sociology of Consumption*. London: Sage.

Eder, K. (2003). "Social movements and democratization," in G. Delanty, & E.F. Isin, (Eds.) *Handbook of Historical Sociology*. London: Sage.

Edmunds, J. and Turner, B.S. (2002). *Generations, Culture and Society*. Buckingham: Open University Press.

Edwards, T. (2000). *Contradictions of Consumption, Concepts, Practices and Politics in Consumer Society*. Buckingham: Open University Press.

Featherstone, M. (1991). *Consumer Culture and Postmodernism*. London: Sage.

Giddens, A. (1991). *Modernity and Self-identity, Self and Society in the Late-modern Age*. Cambridge: Polity.

Gilleard, C. and Higgs, P. (2005). *Context of Ageing*. Cambridge: Polity.

Horowitz, D. (2004). *The Anxieties of Affluence: Critiques of American Consumer Culture, 1939-1979*. MA: University of Massachusetts Press.

Laslett, P. (1996 [1989]). *A Fresh Map of Life, The Emergence of the Third Age*, 2nd Edition. Basingstoke. Hampshire: Macmillan Press Ltd.

Mannheim, K. (1952/1997). "The problem of generations," in M.A. Hardy, (Ed.) *Studying Aging and Social Change*. London: Sage.

Marwick, A. (2003). *British Society since 1945*, 4th Edition. London: Penguin.

Offer, A. (2006). *The Challenge of Affluence: Self Control and Well Being in the United States and Britain since 1950*. Oxford: Oxford University Press.

Putnam, R. (2001). *Bowling Alone*. New York: Simon and Shuster.

Runciman, W.G. (1997). *A Treatise on Social Theory*, Volume 3. Cambridge: Cambridge University Press.

Ryder, N.B. (1965). "The Cohort as a Concept in the Study of Social Change." *American Sociological Review*, 30: 843-61.

Sandbrook, D. (2005). *Never Had it so Good, A History of Britain from Suez to the Beatles*. London: Abacus.

Sandbrook, D. (2006). *White Heat, a History of Britain in the Swinging Sixties*. London: Little, Brown.

Schwartz, B. Ward, A. Monterosso, J. Lyubomirsky, S. White, K., and Lehman, D.R. (2002). "Maximising versus satisficing: Happiness is a matter of choice." *Journal of Personality and Social Psychology*, 83, 5: 117-1197.

Sennett, R. (2006). *The Culture of the New Capitalism*. New Haven, CT: Yale University Press.

Simmel, G. (2004). *The Philosophy of Money*. London: Routledge.

Slater, D. (1999). *Consumer Culture and Modernity*. London: Sage.

Tilly, C. and Tarrow, S. (2007). *Contentious Politics*. Boulder, CO: Paradigm.

Tilly, C. (2004). *Social Movements, 1768-2004*. Boulder, CO: Paradigm.

Trentmann, F. (2004). "Beyond Consumerism: New Historical Perspectives on Consumption." *Journal of Contemporary History*, 39, 3: 373-401.

Turner, B.S. (1998) "Ageing and Generational Conflict: A Reply to Sarah Irwin." *British Journal of Sociology* 49: 299-304.

Turner, B.S. (2002). "Strategic generations: Historical change, literary expression and generational politics," in J. Edmunds, and B.S. Turner, *Generational Consciousness, Narrative and Politics*. Lanham: Rowman & Littlefield.

Veblen, T. (1931 [1899]). *The Theory of the Leisure Class*. New York: Random House.
Warde, A. (2002). "Setting the scene: changing conceptions of consumption," in S. Miles, A. Anderson, and K. Meethan (Eds.), *The Changing Consumer: Markets and Meaning*. London: Routledge.
Weber, M. (1978) [1922]. *Economy and Society, An Outline of Interpretive Sociology*. Berkeley, Los Angeles, London: University of California Press.

Part I

Theoretical Perspectives on Generations and Consumption

Part 1

Historical Perspectives on Generation and Consumption

2

The Third Age: Field, Habitus, or Identity?

Chris Gilleard and Paul Higgs

Introduction

Peter Laslett introduced the idea of "the third age" into social gerontology during the mid-1980s (Laslett, 1987; 1989). Since then, it has become a pivotal concept in debates concerning the social and cultural nature of later life in contemporary Western society (Gilleard and Higgs, 2000; Weiss and Bass, 2002; Biggs, 2005). It remains, however, a term open to different interpretations and any definition of the third age implies its ontology. We propose that rather than treating it as a "new stage of life," as Laslett (1987) did, or dismissing it as a short-hand term for the well-off elderly, as Bury (1998) and Blaikie (2002) have, the third age can be better conceptualized as a cultural field (in Bourdieu's sense of the term) shaped by later life consumption patterns, in which particular actors from particular cohorts participate more heavily than others. The nature and forms of that participation and the differing third age "lifestyles" they support extend and expand the nature and form of the field itself. This is the core premise that this chapter will explore.

In an earlier study, we have argued that attempts to define the third age by its underlying cohort or class composition are inadequate because they fail to locate such structures within a particular generational field (Gilleard and Higgs, 2002). It is the existence of a distinct generational field that makes the third age distinct. This field, we suggest, has its historical origins in the cultural transformation of the 1960s and is intimately linked to the development of mass consumer society. Here we extend this argument, which was originally framed by Mannheim's work on "the problem of generation" (Mannheim, 1997) by linking it to Bourdieu's concepts of "field" and "habitus" (Bourdieu, 1977; 1990).

Generational Units and Generational Fields

For Mannheim, the status of a generation is determined by the confluence of a historical period with a particular cohort, in a particular social context. This confluence creates a "community of location," which forms the necessary *but not sufficient conditions* for realizing a "generational unit." Mannheim notes that a further element is needed—participation in a "common destiny" (Mannheim, 1997: 45-47) which then and only then creates a distinct "generational style" (op. cit., 51-53). For many contemporary writers, baby boomers are just such a generational unit, formed by a community of location—namely membership of a cohort born in the 1940s whose members reached adulthood during the 1960s and who will mostly be retiring during the first decade of the twenty-first century. Their common destiny is to have grown up and grown old in conditions of relative security and increased affluence.

However, Mannheim also cautions against speaking of generations "without any further differentiation . . . jumbling together purely biological phenomena and others which are the product of social and cultural forces . . . thus arriv[ing] at a sort of sociology of chronological tables (*Geschichstabellensoziologie*)" (op. cit., 53). As he put it, "every new departure . . . has to operate *in a given field* which although in constant process of change is capable of description in structural terms" (op. cit., 55, italics in original). It is this last point that the analysts of the baby boom cohort/generation have tended to ignore. Representing the third age as a Mannheimian generational unit structured by birth cohort and historical location, such researchers have paid little attention to the social and cultural dynamics that operate within that "community of location." Hence, the ascription of a cohort/generational identity to a defined population is based upon an incomplete representation of Mannheim's conceptualization of "generation."

Instead of fixating upon cohort analyses, practicing such *Geschichstabellensoziologie,* we have turned to the work of Bourdieu and his concept of the cultural field. We are not the first to seek to improve the sociological understanding of generation by integrating Mannheim's ideas with those of Bourdieu. Edmunds and Turner suggested just such a possibility in their book, *Generations, Culture and Society* that was published in 2002 (Edmunds & Turner, 2002: 116). But it is one thing to suggest such integration; it is another to realize it within a coherent theoretical formulation—a goal that Edmunds and Turner did not attempt. Integrating Bourdieu's concept of field with Mannheim's conceptualization of "generation" provides us with an opportunity to achieve that integration, and in the process to re-conceptualize the third age.

For Bourdieu, the term *cultural field* is an "open concept" whose definition can exist only in relation to a particular theoretical system (Bourdieu and Wacquant, 1992). It is not copyrighted and remains open to alternative uses within alternative theoretical systems. Linking Mannheim's theoretical framework of generational units and generational styles to Bourdieu's concept of a cultural field, the third age can be considered as an example of a *generationally defined* cultural field. It is a field defined by particular cultural practices concerning consumption and later life where particular logics of power and influence operate and determine the nature of the participants and the frameworks of these practices.

The underlying logic of the field is determined by consumption, a post-scarcity consumption that supports the search for distinction and that implicitly or explicitly rejects, denies or marginalizes "old-age." The practices that define this field are the routines of individualized consumption, routines whose function can be defined by or which help support what Foucault has referred to as "technologies of the self" (Foucault, 1988). The logic that operates within the third age is the logic of consumption and the individualization of society's material surplus. The growth in *mass access* to this increasing surplus during the second half of the twentieth century helped promote ideals of personal choice and individualized lifestyle as sources of "virtue." These ideals became dominant signifiers of "the good life" (Schulze, 1997). The subsequent evolution of mass consumer society has exercised a continuing influence upon all those who have grown up and grown old within it, creating what Lisabeth Cohen has referred to as "citizen consumers" (Cohen, 2003) whose participation in consumption has come to symbolize the virtues of choice, self-expression, autonomy, and pleasure that became emblematic of a generation during the "long sixties." These virtues were not, of course, self-selected.

To quote Jenkins, "the existence of a field presupposes and in its functioning creates a belief on the part of participants in the legitimacy and value of the capital which is at stake in the field" (Jenkins, 1992: 85). For Bourdieu, the capital at stake is not just material (at least not in shaping its "conscious collectif") but is equally cultural and social. Within the field marked out by the third age, the dominant form of social capital is derived from extended horizontal networks rather than vertically aligned kinships. The linkages established between friends and "partners" have come to overshadow previously valued vertical forms of social capital based upon kith and kin and the spatially secured bonds of inter-generational solidarity. This does not mean there is no interchange between the generations; there is, of course, but it has become a less salient source of social capital.

Much of the cultural capital of the third age derives from the effective use of leisure—engaging in what Ekerdt (1986) has referred to as the "busy ethic," with its emphasis upon activity, exercise, travel, eating out, self-maintenance, and self-care. Distinction lies less in the area of work, in one's past or present contribution to the social product and more in the area outside work—the creation of symbolically valued lifestyles. Work and leisure have become disconnected. Cultural capital flows more powerfully from the use and quality of individual leisure time than from what work is done and how money is earned. The symbolic forms of capital that are legitimated within this field are those that support an active agentic consumerism, consumption that most expresses choice, autonomy, pleasure, and self-expression. The growing opportunities for personal choice that mass consumer society enables, indeed requires, helps to maintain the continuing expansion of material and cultural capital and its overflow from use value into proliferating systems of distinction. Arenas of choice have expanded well beyond the traditional boundaries of the market and now incorporate aspects of the "life world" previously held to be the preserve of either the family or the state. Within this post-sixties mentality, it is not youth per se that is bought and sold so much as the ideologies of youthfulness, symbolized by the consumerist quartet of virtues identified above—choice, autonomy, pleasure, and self-expression.

Old age—attributed community of "the old"—forms a key boundary marking the limits of third age culture. The third age is defined by both the continuities of choice and the discontinuity of old age. Within the field is a conscious absence of any individualized old age. Old age is rejected as a collective choice because it seems to augur a return to the past. The community of old age threatens to dissolve the lifestyles of autonomous individuals, turning them into an amorphous, collective, mass grave—the burial ground of individuality and choice. Old age is culturally marginalized because those who were old and out-of-date were the others that helped a generation define itself. As the signifier of material and symbolic bankruptcy, old age is simply not a choice.

The conscious absence of old age that defines the outer boundaries of the third age is achieved less by people masking or misrepresenting their chronological age as by denying its structural power. Age is emptied of personal meaning and is treated as "nothing but a number." The sixty-year-old contemplating blepharoplasty or botox injections, the seventy-year-old pondering the merits of vibrators, or the eighty-year-old choosing which degree course to study illustrate just some of the extreme habitus of this cultural field. More common and mundane are the many everyday actions of people over sixty; they go out shopping, book holidays, visit the library or leisure centre, e-mail friends, or get online. The practices arising from such everyday micro-choices constitute the very fabric of the third age.

Generational Habitus

Just as a generational location can be thought of as a *"generational field,"* so can what Mannheim termed generational style be reinterpreted as *"generational habitus."* Another of Bourdieu's "open concepts," habitus refers to a set of mostly unconscious practices and forms of being that arise from and help shape the cultural fields in which they are co-assembled. Bourdieu refers to habitus as "history turned into nature" (Bourdieu, 1977). By this he means that lifestyles and everyday cultural practices embody the history of the field within which they emerged. Since we propose treating the third age as a cultural field emerging from the "cultural revolution" of the 1960s, the origins of a third age habitus must be sought in that period of change.

We have earlier argued that the emerging logic of twentieth-century capital fostered a belief in the importance of consumption and choice. This was first realized during the late 1950s and 1960s with the development of class cutting lifestyles and subcultures, based upon deliberately sought distinctions in dress, music, and entertainment (Hebdige, 1979). These distinctions were explicitly generational. They did not seek to reproduce class, but subvert it. The cultural undermining of the pretensions of the middle classes was paralleled by an equal rejection of the restrictiveness of traditional working-class life. Youth, whether middle or working class, turned its collective back on class culture.

The third vector of practice that helped shape the generational habitus of the third age originated in the discourse of the new social movements with their stress upon personal awareness, cultural autonomy, self-expression, and the symbolic nature of the oppression they faced. Personal choices became political choices, and national liberation movements joined with cultural liberation movements to assert the voice of autonomy and self-expression. Race, gender, sexual orientation, and (for a while) age movements united in a radical front crossing boundaries that had previously gone largely unchallenged. This politics of recognition, as Nancy Fraser has described it, was voiced more by students than by workers—young men and women whose numerical significance became a global phenomenon. For these students, and their youthful counterparts in the arts and the media, self-expression meant the freedom to reject all that was old, all that represented the old way of doing things. Colonial authorities, the political establishment, and the owners of capital symbolized the old and those who were not old, not white, not men, and not masters found common cause in expressing a wish to be heard, a wish to replace old capital with new.

The fourth vector—admittedly a much stronger influence in Europe than in the US—was the transformation of urban life. The clearances of old pre-war inner-city housing stock laid the foundations for new social housing that was designed to house, not just "young families" but families ready to engage with the new technologies of home. The flats and houses of the post war estates that were built in the fifties and sixties were designed with washing machines and tumble driers, vacuum cleaners and TV's, electric irons, and electric cookers in mind. They were designed not to replicate pre-war standards of living, nor to reproduce pre-war styles of living. The new estates that replaced or restructured the old communities of propinquity, created the conditions in which household structures themselves could change. Those aged over sixty were increasingly able to live apart from their children, just as their children were able to live apart from their parents. The generational split that was being created within the arena of fashion, music, and the new media was also being realized at the level of the individual household (Gilleard and Higgs, 2005).

Last, and lagging behind many of these social and cultural changes, work itself began to change. The transformation of working life in post-war, post-industrial Western society began as a cultural shift in attitudes toward work, a shift in perspective made possible by the general rise in living standards and the new stability provided by the post-war welfare state. Despite the continued growth in factories and factory workers, in coal mining, engineering, and shipbuilding, the centrality of the workplace was hollowed out. Migrant workers were brought in to do jobs that the host population was reluctant to do. The pre-war gendered segregation of the workplace was declining and the time spent at work was continuing to shrink. Work was no longer a homogenizing community, nor a place capable of instilling fear and discipline. Expansion in the size of the public sector workforce altered the relationships on the "shop floor." This hollowing out of work as a dominant en-culturing force helped create alternative spaces in which new lifestyles could be fashioned that relied less upon the realities of home or work.

As the influence of work and family on individual lifestyle declined, personal identity became increasingly commodified. Rather than being experienced as a corrupting influence upon youth, the market seemed more like an ally, a radical force opposed by the old guard, the establishment, many of whom seemed to think that the working classes were ill suited to membership of the "leisure classes." Many of the habitus of the third age were formed within these emerging markets and their novel practices of consumption. Consumption as a way of expressing one's identity, of expressing generational defiance, of valorizing what was new and different, and of exercising freedom of choice and self-expression shaped the rules of the field. Personal distinction, self-expression, and individual freedom that were so much vaunted by the youth of the sixties have proved some of the more enduring marketing tropes that are still applied to an ever-increasing array of products and services—ranging from holidays, travel, and clothing to personal pensions, savings accounts, and retirement homes.

The reduction of massive structured inequalities within the population of most Western countries and the corresponding demise of class politics has created an unspoken division between the majority of the population whose individual differentiations are facilitated by access to the market and a variety of marginalized identities that are denied the opportunities of such incorporation. The new politics of social inclusion seek to extend the market to all, or at least seeks to simulate such extension. Those for whom freedom through choice proves incapable of realization within the market are either provided with proxies—advocates and representatives—to enter the market on their behalf or are marginalized as the uncivilized other, who represent a threat to our freedoms, who challenge the inalienability of our right to choose.

Third Age Lifestyles versus Third Age Identities

The distinction between lifestyle and identity is an important element in the shift from first to second modernity, the transition from modern to post-modern cultures. According to Michael Kammen, the term lifestyle first entered Webster's dictionary in 1961, "replac[ing] its predecessors such as 'way of life' and convey[ing] nuances of indeterminate class characteristics" (Kammen, 1999: 243). Lifestyle possesses an element of agency that is missing from the term "identity" where structural processes are privileged. Lifestyle is expressed in choice. It is consciously adopted or imagined and possesses a fluidity that supports, rather than inhibits, change. Identity is ascribed, accepted, or undermined. It is not the consequence of individual actions. Individuals become aware of their identity but do not create it. Identity presumes community, lifestyle, and individuality.

Kammen has described "the swift, full-scale emergence and impact of mass culture" between 1958 and 1967. Over this period, popular music expanded, record labels proliferated, paperbacks, magazines and comics filled the shelves of bookstores, and fashion ceased to be primarily a concern of elites instead becoming a mass preoccupation with a proliferation of boutiques targeting teenagers and young women—complete with an accompanying transformation in men's fashion. TV recruited millions into participating vicariously in mass appeal virtual communities. Market segmentation grew, but it was no longer segmentation based upon an overarching identity or class and helped foster the emergence of popular subcultures. As generational divisions grew more salient, class distinctions became less powerful.

Subsequent decades saw a further loss of definition in the nature of the working class as the nature and organization of work was itself transformed in the wake of the global financial crises of the 1970s. The growth of new social movements further undermined the political centrality of class, as the personal became the political, and protest focused upon an "establishment" that was as much defined by its age, skin color, and gender as by its class representation. The road from class politics, to identity politics, to lifestyle politics may not be quite so linear or so straightforward, but from the vantage point of the beginning of the twenty-first century, it is easier to see just how much the political agenda has changed from the 1950s and the "tragedy" of retirement.

This shift from identity to lifestyle has been reflected in the cultural organization of age and ageing. Age related organizations on both sides of the Atlantic have developed a much more explicit consumerist orientation in their search for customers (e.g., Age Concern, somewhat belatedly, and the AARP much earlier). The rise of self help literature has made ageing a matter of increasing individual responsibility buttressed by more personal advocacy of how individuals and groups have learned to combat the structuring tyrannies of old age (e.g., Zelda Curtis' edited book, *Life After Work*, subtitled *Stories of Freedom, Opportunity and Change* or Carleen Brice's *Age ain't Nothing but a Number.* Curtis, 1998; Brice, 2003). Political attempts to represent the aged as a class have been singularly unsuccessful despite high levels of political participation amongst older people (Binstock, 2000; Gilleard, 2005). What is most relevant about this shift, from the perspective of studying the third age as a cultural field, is that it can be interpreted through the rise and fall of particular lifestyles, displayed in the consumer-oriented choices of individuals without recourse to a collective grouping or classification of those individuals as possessing a "distinct" social identity.

Talking of "third-agers"—a form of discourse into which it is easy to slip—morphs easily into treating the third age as a group defined by their occupying a common life stage. It can seem like simply another way of talking about "late middle age" (Twigg, 2003)—though talking of "late middle age" is itself another distinctive discourse of our times. Talking of third age lifestyles, or ways of participating in the third age rather than "third agers," helps retain the sense of fluidity that is needed to avoid reification of terms that are (as Bourdieu said) essentially "open concepts." This approach toward the third age enables the study of ageing to be more than the study of those we deem aged. It permits us to consider the structures of power and influence that shape the cultural fields of ageing. This includes not only the various forms of capitalism currently operating within the market (particularly retail and financial capital) but also the role of social policy, technology, mass culture, and cultural globalization—based on the logic underlying the ideologies of autonomy and choice that make up "modernity two" (Beck et al., 2003).

Figure 2.1
Cohort Analyses to Test Key Hypotheses about the Third Age

Comparisons of those born in the 1920s with those born in the 1940s will show that members of the latter cohort are characterized by more:

- Economic, social, cultural, and physical differentiation
- Salience of horizontal (partner, peer relationship, and friendship) networks
- Desire and support for personal autonomy, choice, and freedom of expression
- Resistance to an identity as "old," "aged," or "elderly"
- Involvement in a wider range of leisure pursuits
- Diversity in sources of income and expenditure
- Lifestyles unrestricted by gendered expectations
- Willingness to discard what is old—clothes, furnishings, household goods, décor, etc.
- Extensive use of nutraceuticals and cosmaceuticals
- Time spent "shopping" and a greater range of venues where "shopping" takes place
- Time spent on and greater distances traveled when "holidaying"
- Ownership of property at home and abroad and of other forms of wealth
- Detachment from the local neighborhood
- Engagement with domestic information and communication technologies

The Significance of Cohort

Just as lifestyles have replaced identities, so habits of consumption have replaced the habits of the workplace. Communities are no longer identified with local workplaces, retirement is no longer a gendered transition from a valued to a valueless status, and post-working life is about more than managing day-to-day life. Most people aged sixty and over can now hope to avoid, or at least defer, becoming enmeshed in the ascribed identities of old age.[1] This transformation in later life has become more evident within the last twenty-five years. It has affected only a minority of those born in the 1920s, more of those born in the 1930s, most of those who were born in the 1940s, and probably nearly all of those born in the 1950s. To the extent that the third age has emerged during a particular period in history, it is inevitable that members of particular birth cohorts will be most closely identified with and will be bigger players in its particular cultural field. In that sense, at least, a cohort is a significant delineator of the third age.

Consequently, one can explore potential inter-cohort differences in social and cultural behavior while still considering the third age as a cultural field. For example, one can predict that later cohorts, those born in the 1940s and 1950s, will have experienced a greater generational divide between themselves and their parents compared with earlier cohorts, particularly those born in the 1910s and 1920s. Similar inter-cohort differences can be predicted—such as greater post retirement discretionary expenditure, more active habits of resistance to the identities of old age, greater support for personal liberty, greater support for freedom of expression and less trust in authority, greater variety in leisure time activities and in retirement income, more and more varied forms of personal wealth (in terms of property and financial investments) and less gendered lifestyles. Some of the more important hypotheses concerning the third age can be explored through cohort analysis, as illustrated in Figure 2.1 below.

Such predicted differences help delineate those who are or who are not active participants in "third age"; later born cohorts will have more members whose habitus power and status reflects this cultural field. More sixty-plus people born in the 1940s will "articulate" the features of the third age than sixty-plus-year-olds born in the 1920s and 1930s. But as ever cohort, period, and age remain confounded and the salience of cohort can always be reinterpreted as a combination of period and life stage. Rather than enter such debates, it is more fruitful to explore the identity of the field through the observable habitus of those who inhabit it—in short to explore the "cultures of ageing" rather than the ageing of cohorts, focusing upon actions rather than actors, modes of speech rather than speakers, and practices rather than practitioners. Cohort analysis is one means of exploration of these cultures, but it will always be a potentially dangerous, double-edged tool.

Conclusion

It may be helpful to conclude by stating first what the third age is not. First, we do not conceive of it as a form of identity conferred by being a member of a particular birth cohort. Nor do we think it a newly discovered stage of life or a cultural identity created by the media or the market. Equally, we do not think it will advance our understanding by reading the third age as a status conferred by a combination of chronological age and ownership of a particular amount of physical, financial, and cultural capital. While all these factors are relevant to understanding the logic of the third age, they do not define it because they treat it as a status given to some individuals and not others, a structuring of difference between individuals and between groups. We prefer to view the third age in a cultural sense, as something that is revealed in lifestyles rather than through structured identities, lifestyles that operate within and that help give definition to an emerging cultural field that has been historically formed by the emergence of mass culture and mass affluence. They are realized through a consciousness that sought to separate itself from the mentality of an earlier generation and supported by lifestyle choices that resist, and by resisting undermine, the structuring identity of old age. Of course, the third age is itself changing as the participants of the field change and as technology and the institutional forms of global capital evolve. Whether one emphasizes the opportunities presented by the third age for a new agency in later life or berates the corrosiveness of the culture that creates it and the illusions and false consciousness that it supports may be as much a matter of personality as it is of theoretical depth.

The work of Bourdieu and Mannheim help give a structure for understanding the third age in this way, but the simple act of invoking their names and using their terms does not determine the value of such a formulation. For this to be realized there needs to be both ongoing debate; further cultural and social analysis; and, *pace* earlier criticisms, a continuing engagement with *Geschichstabellensoziologie*.

Note

1.   By which we mean the majority of people in Western societies do not now expect to face of either poverty or institutionalization, nor be dependent upon means-tested welfare after passing their sixtieth birthday (see Gilleard and Higgs, 2005, for the evidence supporting this claim).

References

Beck, U., Bonss, W., and Lau, C. (2003). "The theory of reflexive modernisation: Problematic, hypotheses and research programme." *Theory Culture & Society*, 20: 1-33.

Biggs, S. (2005). "Beyond Appearances: Perspectives on Identity in Later Life and Some Implications for Method." *The Journals of Gerontology Series B: Psychological Sciences and Social Sciences,* 60: S118-S128.

Binstock, R.H. (2000). "Older people and voting participation: past and future." *The Gerontologist*, 40: 18-31.

Blaikie, A. (2002). "The secret world of sub-cultural ageing: What unites and what divides?" in (Ed.) L. Andersson, *Cultural Gerontology* (pp. 95-110). Westport, CT: Auburn House.

Bourdieu, P. (1977). *Outline of a Theory of Practice.* Cambridge: Cambridge University Press.

Bourdieu, P. (1990). *The Logic of Practice.* Cambridge, Polity Press.

Bourdieu, P. and Wacquant, L.J.D. (1992). *An Invitation to Reflexive Sociology.* Cambridge: Polity Press.

Brice, C. (Ed.). (2003). *Age ain't Nothing but a Number.* London: Souvenir Press.

Bury, M. (1998). "Ageing, gender and sociological theory," in (Eds.) S. Arber and J. Ginn, *Connecting Gender and Ageing* (pp. 15-29). London: Sage Publications.

Cohen, L. (2003). *A Consumers' Republic: The Politics of Mass Consumption in Postwar America.* New York, Alfred A. Knopf.

Curtis, Z. (Ed.) (1999). *Life After Work.* London: The Women's Press.

Ekerdt, D. J. (1986). "The busy ethic: moral continuity between work and retirement." *The Gerontologist,* 26: 239-244.

Foucault, M. (1988) "Technologies of the self," in (Eds.) L.H. Martin, H. Guttman, and P.H. Hutton, *Technologies of the Self: A Seminar with Michel Foucault.* London: Tavistock Publications.

Gilleard, C. (2005). "The power of silver: Age and identity politics," paper presented at the VIIth European Sociological Association Conference. Torun, Poland, September 9-12th.

Gilleard, C. and Higgs, P. (2000). *Cultures of Ageing: Self, Citizen and the Body.* London: Prentice Hall.

Gilleard, C. and Higgs, P. (2002). "The Third Age: Class, Cohort or Generation?" *Ageing and Society,* 22: 369-382.

Gilleard, C. and Higgs, P. (2005). *Contexts of Ageing: Class, Cohort and Community.* Cambridge: Polity Press.

Hebdige, D. (1979). *Subculture: The Meaning of Style.* London: Methuen.

Jenkins, R. (1992). *Pierre Bourdieu,* London: Routledge.

Kammen, M. (1999). *American Culture, American Tastes: Social change and the 20th Century,* New York: Basic Books.

Laslett, P. (1987). "The emergence of the Third Age," *Ageing & Society,* 7: 113-160.

Laslett, P. (1989). *A Fresh Map of Life.* London: Weidenfeld & Nicolson.

Lord, M.G. (2004). *Forever Barbie.* New York: Walker and Company.

Mannheim, K. (1997) "The problem of generations," in (Ed.) M.A. Hardy, *Studying Aging and Social Change: Conceptual and Methodological Issues* (pp. 22-65). London: Sage Publications.

Marwick, A. (1998). *The Sixties.* Oxford: Oxford University Press.

Schulze, G. (1997). "From situations to subjects: moral discourse in transition," in (Eds.) P. Sulkunen, J. Holmwood, H. Radner, and G. Schulze, *Constructing the New Consumer Society* (pp. 38-57). London: Macmillan.

Twigg, J. (2003). "The body, gender and age: Feminist insights in social gerontology," *Journal of Aging Studies* 18: 59-73.

Weiss, R.S. and Bass, S.A. (2002). *Challenges of the Third Age: Meaning and Purpose in Later Life.* Oxford, Oxford University Press.

3

Goods Not Gods: New Spiritualities, Consumerism, and Religious Markets

Bryan S. Turner

Introduction: The Economics of Scarcity

While religion has been much discussed by economic historians and sociologists in relation to industrialization and the rise of capitalist society within the framework of Max Weber's sociology of religion, the relationship between religions, consumer society, and consumer behavior has received much less attention. The main exception is Colin Campbell's *The Romantic Ethic and the Spirit of Modern Consumerism,* which located the cultural roots of modern consumerism in Pietism and the romantic movement. Paradoxically of course, Karl Marx (1965) had employed a variety of religious metaphors in *The German Ideology* of 1845 to describe commodity relations in terms of transcendence, community, and experience. The most famous was his metaphor of the fetishism of commodities in which commodified objects appear to take on an objective life of their own (Richards, 1991: 68-9). In historical terms, the Victorian period was one in which there did indeed appear to be a close relationship between Christianity, colonialism, and the growth of world capitalism. Henry Stanley had in his *In Darkest Africa* (1890) celebrated the inevitable spread of Christianity on the back of British commodities. Similarly, the spread of Christianity to Southeast Asia would not have occurred without the help of the Dutch East India Company. There appears to be some general historical evidence that in Africa and America itinerant preachers were often itinerant peddlers (Giggie, 2006).

Despite these obvious historical illustrations, the recent growth in the sociology of consumption has taken place largely without any theoretical reflection on the issue of consumerism and religion or without much empirical research on religion as consumption. In a collection of papers on *Consumption Matters* (1996) Pnina Werbner offered an analysis of Christmas that rejected the view that Christmas is simply a consumer orgy that above all celebrates modern consumerism. She argued that Christmas, in fact, is based on unilinear gift giving (from old to young and from rich to poor) which legitimizes hierarchical forms of power expressed through the domination of symbolic violence. In global terms, however, Christmas now plays an important commercial role in many societies that are formally secular. In Singapore, which is constitutionally a secular state, a thoroughgoing syncretism of religious and secular symbols is used to sell Christmas goods. There appears to be general agreement among historians and sociologists that there is an important connection between new patterns of subjectivity and the rise of consumerism (Trentmann, 2006)

In the 1990s, there was little interest in or awareness of the growth of religious markets on the part of sociologists (Warde, 1996). This lack of interest has persisted despite the very obvious growth, at least in the United States, of drive-in churches, drive-through confessions, religious films, inspirational literature and religious bookstalls, and devotional objects including jewelry. In short, "Spirituality, like hamburgers, was increasingly something one could get quickly and in a variety of places" (Wuthnow, 2003: 98). This commercialization of Christianity has been matched globally by the growth in worldwide sales of Buddhist amulets, texts, and services and the global development of yoga as a therapeutic practice that can be completely divorced from its philosophical underpinnings. There is growing anthropological evidence of widespread commodification of religions in Asia through pilgrimages, religious sites, and personal services (Kitiarsa, 2007). However, these changes are merely superficial evidence of a more profound change in the very character of modern culture and the economy.

In contemporary sociology of religion, there has been considerable interest in the idea of religious markets and the application of rational choice theories to the "economics" of religious behavior. In this discussion, I want to consider the differentiation of this global religious market and the complex relationships—both antagonistic and co-operative—that exist between religion and consumerism. In particular, I want to consider the global production of religion as lifestyle and the commodification of religious services, practices, and goods within a consumer society. If Weber discovered asceticism as the "economic ethic" of industrial capitalism, can there be a religiously inspired hedonistic ethic of consumerism? Is an ethic of life affirmation rather than life denial the appropriate Weberian ethic of modern consumerism? Does the shift from saving to spending represent a shift in terms of William James's notion of "varieties of religious experience" from the "sick soul" to the "religion of healthy-mindedness" (James, 1922). These issues in contemporary religious orientations are explored partly by developing Daniel Bell's original insight into the paradoxical relations between production and consumption in *The Cultural Contradictions of Capitalism* (1976).

Classical economics was built on the assumption of scarcity and, hence, economics is essentially the science concerned with fitting scarce means to desirable ends (Turner and Rojek, 2001). Economizing behavior requires the rational allocation of means to ends in a condition of general scarcity. Classical political economy held to the view that nature was niggardly, paradoxically providing humans with abundant desires and limited means. Unfortunately, because life is characterized by its inescapable natural scarcity, desires have to be curtailed and expectations restrained. The asceticism of the Protestant sects, as described classically in Max Weber's *The Protestant Ethic and the Spirit of Capitalism*, represented a rational orientation to scarcity, in which the rational actor is one who saves against future adversity by limiting his or her contemporary consumption. Classical economics also assumed the existence of a negative relationship between population growth and economic wealth, as presented most notoriously in Thomas Malthus's *Essay on the principle of population* of 1798. We should remember that Malthus wrote the essay against what he regarded as the false doctrine of happiness explicit in the enlightenment theories of Condorcet. In the past, the human condition required saving, frugality, and prudence and, therefore, in traditional societies the relationship between resources (especially the food supply) and life expectancy was, more or less, regulated by a Malthusian logic. He argued that, given the sexual drive, the need for food, and the declining yield of the soil, the increase in population would inevitably supersede the food supply. Population increase could either be controlled by positive means (such as famine, disease, and war) or by preventive means (such as vice, chastity, and late marriage). Any attempt to improve the living conditions of the working class could not be sustained in the long term, because such reforms would increase the population, thereby reducing living standards by reducing the food supply.

The result has been that economics has found it difficult to develop a robust theory of consumption and consumer behavior, because it has difficulty in conceptualizing long-term abundance and unlimited gratification. Shaking off the legacy of scarcity as a presupposition of economic rationality has been difficult to achieve, and to some extent post-war sociology has filled the gap in trying to understand consumerism as culture and consumer behavior as a set of cultural practices. Early social theories that did have something to say about consumption saw it in largely negative and critical terms. The negative features of consumer concern for social status were clearly expressed by Thorstein Veblen (1994) who published the classic *Theory of the Leisure Class* in 1899. He described a world in which the traditional values of Puritanism were turned upside down by waste and luxury. Similarly, the Frankfurt School critique of (American) consumerism interpreted consumerism as a mechanism for neutralizing any criticism of capitalist exploitation. Theodor Adorno, in *The Culture Industry* (1991), provided a comprehensive critique of the fetishism of culture, the fascist tendencies of modern America, in which mass society and mass consumption created an inauthentic culture promoting the passivity of the working class.

Similarly, with the growth of corporate America, the organization man was tied to the company and occupied a domestic space that equally promoted conformity. In *The Organization Man,* W. H. Whyte (1956) showed how conformist values in the organization also had implications for domestic life and gender relationships. Company wives were expected to be pretty, but not too sexy, and ambitious, but not blatantly materialistic. The organization culture of the 1950s suburbia created what came to be called "lifestyle"—in which the organization couple progressed from a two-bedroom court apartment to a three-bedroom house and subsequently through various stages of ranch houses, split-level accommodation, and finally (as retirement approaches) back into a two-bedroom apartment. Women were trapped in this consumer lifestyle and their physical slenderness was intended to express corporate values. The social ethic or organization man spilled over into their leisure activities. Personal saving had lost its moral imperative, and young couples now saved for specific items—houses, cars, or schooling—that would give their lives more security and stability. Attendance at the local church and concern for the education of their children were key elements in the stability of their personal lives, which in other respects were characterized by transience as the management posted them to new branches of the organization.

More recent theories of consumption; such as Pierre Bourdieu's work on distinction, cultural capital, fields, and competition; have in many respects been equally negative. In Bourdieu's *Distinction* (1984) the competitive struggle between different class fractions is manifested at the level of individual taste and the consumption of commodities. Individual dispositions are expressed in terms of preferences for items of consumer culture and activities such as popular sports. The interpretations of Bourdieu's theory of consumption have been quite divergent (Fowler, 1997: 8-9). His work has been seen as a celebration of working-class taste because he shows that high culture is equally determined by competition between elites. Other critics suggest that his attempt to give adequate weight to the idea of strategic practices failed because the legacy of Marxist materialism was not transformed and his work was thus profoundly reductionistic. There is also the view that his theory is specific to French conditions and cannot be generalized (Edmunds and Turner, 2002a). In political terms, since Bourdieu was an implacable critic of neo-liberalism, he was by definition hostile to the world of advertising, consumerism, easy credit, and "leisure" (Callewaert, 2006).

In these sociological approaches to consumerism, there is a persistent if uneven theme which is that "honest toil" in productive activities is worthwhile and morally defensible, whereas consumption is morally questionable. From this perspective, the knowledge society that appears to do away with industrial production, the factory, and labor must be an artificial society that keeps the masses entertained with pure spectacle. Insofar as in the advanced world fundamental "needs" have been satisfied, modern consumption is about expressive needs and symbolic activities. The whole tradition of socialism, of which I assume Bourdieu is clearly a part, has emphasized the dignity of labor as well as its drudgery. By contrast, the leisure time that was available to the bourgeoisie was morally corrosive, being grounded in a life that was somehow inauthentic. Jean Baudrillard, in a series of publications such as *The Mirror of Production* (1973), described the failure of Marxism to grasp the social significance of the decline of industrial capitalism and the growth of consumerism. In the economy of signs, the social field is an ensemble of simulations that are endlessly self-referential. As the world of signs becomes increasingly divorced from reality, it is hyper-real or post-modern, and the social world becomes a Disneyland in which (as in America) everything is a fake (Baudrillard, 1986). Perhaps one of the few sociologists to take a more subtle and complex view of the cultural ambiguities and paradoxes of consumerism was Bell. In *The Cultural Contradictions,* he argued that the hedonism that was required in a consumer society was incompatible with the rationality that was required to sustain the economic conditions of modern production. According to Bell, the credit card has given us instant gratification and hedonism has promoted the idea of pleasure as a way of life.

The Theology of Unhappiness: Scarcity and Salvation

From this brief overview, we can conclude that scarcity has been a basic assumption of political economy in defining what is to count as moral behavior, namely, behavior that is careful and cautious, not given over to indulgence or living beyond our means. These assumptions have also been important in Christian asceticism in the criticism of greed and sloth. We might plausibly argue that the seven deadly sins promoted a moral system relevant to a world of scarcity. Given the ever-present threat of famine, feasting and excess were inevitable counterparts. Utopian visions of plenty and abundance were set against the real world of uncertainty and privation. The medieval imaginary land of Cockaigne—possibly derived from "cake land"—was a world of luxury and idleness. By contrast, medieval saints were typically recognized and celebrated for their abstinence and ascetic behavior. The sanctity of Joan of Arc was measured by her abstinence, by her ascetic diet, and by her lack of menstruation; these physical phenomena of bodily denial defined her virginity. The Maid was constructed as the suffering of France and as a parallel being to the suffering Christ (Warner, 1981).

There has been a longstanding relationship between what we might call a theology of unhappiness and the secular doctrine of scarcity. In traditional Christianity, life on earth was merely a prelude to eternal life for those who have been saved or to eternal punishment for the wicked. As a millenarian movement, the theology of the early Christian community had little interest in this world and, therefore, there was little purpose to saving or to investing in this world. The abundance the New Testament promises to mankind is in the next world, not in this one. Christian asceticism could be said to be, in this sense, premised on a theology of unhappiness but with the promise of lasting happiness in heaven. R.H. Tawney (1926: 31) reminds us in *Religion and the Rise of Capitalism* that medieval writers on economic theory accepted two basic assumptions: economic interests were subordinate to the real business of life on earth, which is salvation, and that economic conduct was subordinate to moral teaching. The church fathers were critical of usury, lotteries, excessive profits, and unfair trading practices. Against this medieval background, Weber's Protestant ethic thesis is famous for its account of how the Protestant sects came to sanction wealth that had arisen for productive toil, but this "economic ethic" did not sanction wastefulness, luxury, or consumption, especially where it was associated with personal adornment. John Wesley was famous for saying that Methodists should earn all they could, save all they could and give all they could away (in charitable acts). Consequently, Wesley banned women from his chapels if they displayed their wealth and status through jewelry or other signs of luxury.

Consumerism has been regarded generally as a corrosive force undermining commitment to a religious interpretation of the world and competing with religious institutions by attracting youth groups to a consumer paradise. The great transformation of modern religions—and thus the principal thesis of this essay—is that contemporary mainstream Christianity has quietly but uniformly abandoned its original theology of death, the life to come, and the doctrine of redemption from sin, and has had to adjust itself to a modern world in which there is an expectation of abundance, the endless satisfaction of desires, the creation of new needs through advertising, and the democratization of consumerism through easy credit, mortgages, and low interest rates. It also exists in a world where therapeutic stem-cell research holds out the promise of prolongevity. Religion has to make the shift from a message of salvation in a context of scarcity, to a theology of abundance with an emphasis on happiness now.

In traditional cultures, religion often promised material rewards to its members. These are often referred to as "prosperity cults," which were particularly attractive to the poor in offering gifts from heaven for simple adherence and belief. These prosperity cults were the product of scarcity and the unpredictable character of human life, but the challenge for mainstream theology today is also to come to terms with a secular life of unlimited consumer desires and the expectations of immediate satisfaction. Life on earth is no longer merely a prelude to the consumption of happiness in the next world; the promise of consumerism is to have one's desires satisfied now. Why invest in a theology of unhappiness when eternal bliss beckons us in the immediate world of consumer objects?

Modern churches have made some significant changes to come to terms with these new conditions. In the United States, many black churches whose congregations suffer from poverty and neglect have openly embraced a doctrine of health and wealth in which salvation means good fortune in this life. These benefits are immediately available and for little effort. Demands for this worldly blessing can be satisfied in popular religion simply by offering a Seven Lifetime Prayer request to a pastor like Pat Robertson, who will enter this request in the prayer room of the Christian Broadcasting Network (CBN) where thousands of these requests for success are lodged (Bruce, 1990). The promise of wealth and health has an obvious attraction to the poor who have missed out in the American dream.

While Christian churches can respond to affluence by developing techniques and ideas that are compatible with consumerism, there remain some profound tensions between the inherited theology of the Abrahamic religions and modernity, but consumerism may be equally challenging to many of the assumptions of sociology, especially Marxist social theory. Within the context of British sociology, the much-lamented decline of the strong program of social class analysis has been closely related to the growth of affluence and consumerism and the decline of traditional labor politics (Crompton, 1996). New Labour can be regarded as the political indicator of working-class embourgeoisement, the decline of trade unionism, and the erosion of social-class identities. The decline of class politics has been matched by the growth of culture as the "true" marker of social position. Alongside the growth of cultural services in the modern economy, in the universities cultural studies emerged out of academic debates in departments of English literature over the established canon. *The Uses of Literacy* (Hoggart, 1957) and *Culture and Society* (Williams, 1958) were major contributions to the study, not only of literature, but also of British society. The theme of these studies was the loss of working-class community, the rise of consumer society, and the dominance of middle-class privacy and individualism. Hoggart and Williams lamented the decline of the co-operative tradition of working-class autonomy, the transformation of the culture of northern cities like Leeds and

Sheffield by television and consumerism, and the trivialization of both popular and serious culture. These northern cities had also been the home of fundamentalist Protestantism and evangelism—for example, the Assemblies of God, the Salvation Army, and the Methodists—which also preached a message of honesty and teetotalism against the temptations of the pub, the club, and the football stadium (Wilson, 1961). Such forms of evangelical religion were seen in some sense to be "true" expressions of working-class consciousness because there was an affinity between the "respectable poor" and the evangelical churches. While in northern cities working-class chapels were relatively popular, working-class culture in London was largely indifferent to both Christianity and socialism in the late nineteenth-century and up to the Second World War (Meacham, 1977). Consumerism is obviously closely connected with income, but it does not solidify, as it were, into a class consciousness.

The post-war generations lived through the Cold War and came to maturity in conditions of growing affluence, the decline of the trade unions, and the erosion of social class as the most important marker of identity (Edmunds and Turner, 2002b). While these generations were always threatened by potential disaster, such as nuclear war during the Kennedy confrontation with Khrushchev, they lived in retrospect under conditions of relative peace. Military conscription, the rationing of essential household items of clothing and food, barrack room drill and the sheer cultural boredom of the 1950s had come to an end. In international terms, Aden, Suez, Kenya, and the Malaysian emergency were military episodes that marked the decline of British military power. The Suez crisis of 1956 demonstrated that Britain could no longer operate as a great power without American support and approval, and Britain subsequently withdrew from any further significant colonial adventures (including Mrs. Thatcher's defense of British interests in the south Atlantic in the Falklands War in 1982). The pragmatism of Harold Macmillan; whose colonial policies allowed Britain to avoid the confrontations that dominated such colonial powers as France, Portugal, and Belgium in the post-war period; made the decline of Britain less painful than the colonial decline of other European societies. In short, modern sociology has to be understood in terms of the rise and decline of the baby boomers and their emergence out of post-war austerity into late century affluence.

Much social and cultural critique of consumerism continues, therefore, to be based on the idea of the dignity of labor, the importance of industrial production over financial services, and the idea that a consumer reality is a false, simulated, and inauthentic reality. Social and political critical theory is based implicitly on a socio-theology of labor. The critique of leisure society is also invariably elitist. From the perspective of the Left, one aspect of the problem of the critique of consumption has been the strength of the economic boom from 1950 to the late 1970s, when per capita growth in Europe rose from 1 percent per annum to 4 percent and mass unemployment disappeared with unemployment rates falling from around 8 percent to less than 2 percent. Whereas John Maynard Keynes had argued that the problem of interwar economics was the "stickiness" of money that is people's reluctance to part with it, advertising helped people to feel comfortable with the conversion of desire into purchase. Consumerism brought about a greater degree of social equality as holidays, homes, washing machines, and motorcars became more widely affordable. The result has been a social revolution:

> Capitalism's success eroded class rivalries and replaced the activist and utopian mass politics of the inter-war era with a more bloodless politics of consumption and management. Goods not gods were what people wanted. (Mazower, 1998: 306)

If consumerism does not need gods, it also tends to be a post-heroic era; giving rise to what elsewhere I have called "passive" generations (Edmunds and Turner, 2002c). If post-war student activism gave rise to CND, anti-apartheid movements, and eventually to the events of 1968, the era of consumerism was the era of Generation X (Turner, 2005). However, the apparent loss of heroic political activity has been true of both East and West. In Eastern Europe, communist authorities were alarmed by the cynicism and disaffection of the post-revolutionary generations or "hero's children," as Paul Neuburg (1972) called them. One aspect of religious evangelism and renewal is the quest to sustain commitment among young generations, especially in a period of affluence. This quest for commitment is characteristic of Pentecostalism as well as of modern reformist Islam.

Secularization and Religious Consumption: Two Illustrations

There are obviously porous boundaries between religious fiction and religious fact. Films and popular fiction compete spiritually and culturally for the "religious imaginary" in ways that professional religious intellectuals and institutions find hard to comprehend, even less to control. To illustrate these issues, we might briefly compare two recent but very different examples from popular culture, namely, Dan Brown's *The Da Vinci Code* that came out in 2003 and Mel Gibson's *The Passion of the Christ* that was launched on February 25, 2004. The former irritated the authorities within the Catholic Church, because it appeared that many lay people were attempting to follow the trail for the Holy Grail in imitation of the novel's main story line. Brown's book (and subsequent film version) became the target of scholarly criticisms (Bock, 2004). Both have enjoyed globally large sales, despite the apparent artistic failure of *The Da Vinci Code* as a film. Nine months after the book appeared, there were 4.5 million copies in print. Brown's other novels have subsequently been enjoying substantial sales. *The Passion* was also a major commercial success. Within two months of its release, it had generated box-office receipts of around $387 million. The film was directly promoted at the grassroots by ministers of Evangelical Churches, conservative Roman Catholics, and Charismatics. This mass-marketing strategy had the support of local church leaders who encouraged their congregations to attend, often through block-booking tickets. The film was also promoted through various ancillary markets. More than one million "witness cards" were printed and circulated in support of the evangelical aspect of the film. The soundtrack was promoted by Sony Music and Integrity Music. Four million copies of the film were sold on the first day of its release and *The Passion Photography* from the movie has gone into its eight printing and sold over 650,000 copies.

Brown's book, by contrast, is controversial as a challenge to Christian, especially Catholic orthodoxy. For instance, many of the claims made within the book have some affinity with scholarly arguments from within feminism and feminist theology about the subordination of feminist themes within traditional Christian theology. Feminist criticism of the patriarchal assumptions of Christian theology have had a long history from Simone de Beauvoir, Carol Christ, and Mary Daly to Julia Kristeva; and in *The Da Vinci Code* these feminist themes became one aspect of Brown's successful novel. By contrast, *The Passion* was designed to be staunchly compatible with orthodox Catholicism, but it too caused public controversy, mainly around accusations of anti-Semitism. These controversies were fanned in 2006 by police charges brought against Gibson for driving under the influence of alcohol and the use of offensive, anti-Semitic language during his encounter with traffic police. Gibson's subsequent apology to the Jewish community did not appear wholly plausible.

What these have in common is the representation of religion as a powerful dimension of popular imagination, but they are also popular representations that circulate as commodities outside the official religious domain and, hence, outside the control of religious authorities. Popular culture constantly appropriates religious symbols and themes, but these commercial developments are paradoxical, because they both contribute to the circulation of religious phenomena and, at the same time, they challenge traditional, hierarchical forms of religious authority. In early 2007, the debate around Brown's book underwent a further development when Canadian documentary filmmaker Simcha Jacobovici claimed to have discovered two ossuaries containing the bones of Jesus of Nazareth and his wife Mary Magdalene. These boxes were made from Jerusalem limestone and originally discovered in 1980 in the suburbs of Talpiyot, but stimulated little significant interest among archaeologists. An inscription on one of the ossuaries—*Mariamene e Mara*—has been translated as "Mary Magdalene the Master." Mr Jacobovici has created a film entitled *The Jesus Family Tomb* with James Cameron the maker of the blockbuster *Titanic*. The film caused immediate offence to the Catholic Church which dismissed these claims as a "Titanic fraud" and there was similar condemnation in Israel, especially from the guardians of the Holy Tomb.

The debate about *The Da Vinci Code* illustrates how fact and fiction become blended in consumer culture and how popular culture can successfully employ and exploit high-culture issues and idioms. Madonna, in many ways, is the principal example of these developments since she is simultaneously an ironic and iconic figure (Hulsether, 2000). Her apparent switch from Catholic themes as Madonna to Jewish mysticism (Kabbalah) as Rachel is characteristic of the fluidity of commitment and identity in popular religion. Of course, Gibson, unlike Brown, had sought the approval of religious leaders before shooting and releasing his film, but he cannot control the unintended consequences of the film once it is in circulation.

While popular religion corrodes the formal authority of official religious institutions often by simply bypassing them, *The Passion* belongs to a traditional and well-established genre of popular, commercial representations of Christ in postcards, domestic paintings, and films. In this sense, there may be nothing particular "new" about popular religion. Before turning to an elaboration of these issues in popular religion, we need to consider how sociologists have recently approached these issues.

The New Paradigm in the Sociology of Religion

In response to these changes in contemporary religion—the growth of de-institutionalized religiosity, the spread of popular religion, Pentecostalism, charismatic movements, the emphasis on personal religious experience, and the growth of fundamentalism—a new paradigm has in the last two decades been promoted in American sociology of religion, variously referred to as the new paradigm, the religious markets approach, or the economic interpretation of religion. Associated with figures such as Rodney Stark, Roger Finke, Laurence Iannaccone, and R. Stephen Warne, this "new" approach is often contrasted disparagingly with "old" European theories of religion. This disparaging tone pervades the debate about these paradigms and they will not easily go away. European sociology, it is alleged, has been too much focused on the meaning that social actors require to make sense of life, and by contrast the new paradigm is concerned with the "economic" dimensions of religious behavior, including both demand for and supply of religious beliefs, practices, and objects.

The critical commentary on European social theory is probably misguided. For example, one of the most influential analyses of the American denominational market was provided by a European aristocrat in the 1840s. Alexis de Tocqueville was struck forcibly by the extraordinary religiosity of the American colonies during his famous journeys around the new society. In his *Democracy in America* (1835-1840), Tocqueville was concerned to understand the reconciliation of popular religiosity and democracy. While in Catholic France the relation between church and state had produced endless and often bloody conflict, in America the moral force of popular religion was important in creating social harmony. Tocqueville was not so much interested in the meaning of religion or in its truth or falsity, but in the social and political benefits that flowed from this unusually robust commitment to religious institutions. Later European visitors including Max Weber and Ernst Troeltsch were equally struck by this contrast between secular Europe and the religiosity of America. Weber arrived in 1904 for the World Congress of Arts and Science in St. Louis and published an article in 1906 on the "churches and sects of North America" (Loader and Alexander, 1985). Tocqueville's analysis has, of course, been transformed by subsequent emphasis on the role of religious pluralism, self-realization, individualism, and voluntary association membership as manifestations of the democratic revolution—as essentially the democratization of religion (Wolin, 2001). The assumption that everybody has religious opinions and that all opinions are equally valid has produced the American religious marketplace, where priestly authority and ecclesiastical hierarchy do not find comfortable locations. In this sense, Methodism—with its commitment to the priesthood of all believers, lay participation, emotional subjectivity, and congregational autonomy—is the harbinger of religious modernization, the logical outcome of which is the proposition that everybody has his or her own personal religion. The competitive American religious market—itself a product of the democratization of popular culture—paved the way for global popular religion as manifest in TV evangelism, lay preaching, the mega-church, and religious advertising. These developments were often regarded by (European) sociologists of religion as a form of secularization, if not the debasement of religion (Wilson, 1966) but they could equally be regarded as instances of the successful adjustment of Christianity to popular culture.

What does the new paradigm claim to be? First, whereas traditional European social theory had emphasized the centrality of secularization to modernization, the new paradigm takes note of the resilience of religion, not only in the United States but globally. Secularization for Wilson and others is an inevitable outcome of modernization, and popular religious movements convince them that the contents of religion is being corroded and eroded by the adoption of popular cultural idioms and practices—such as pop music in religious worship. Second, the new model directs research attention towards the function of religious or spiritual markets in which there is a competition for "brand loyalty" from consumers of religious meaning, practices, and objects. The notion of spiritual markets has been explored empirically and systematically by, for example, Wade Roof in his *Spiritual Marketplace* (1999). We can only understand religion in contemporary America by taking into account the impact of the "baby boomers" on religious practice and consciousness. Roof made an important contribution to the study of religion and generational change in his *A Generation of Seekers* (Roof, 1993), in which the post-war generations were religious seekers, but basically eclectic in their religious "tastes." Religious preferences for lifestyles and consumer objects (religious literature, clothing, holidays, and sacred signs such as the cross) are not different from other cultural markets. The "culture wars" of the post-war period re-organized the map of mainstream religion in North America just as it challenged establishment culture generally. The boundaries of popular religion are constantly redrawn under the impact of large post-war generations, facilitated by an expanding religious marketplace. American denominational pluralism is a spiritual marketplace that, in the constitutional absence of an established church, encourages organizational innovation and cultural entrepreneurship.

The market for religious innovations is a response to massive social change in contemporary America in which an expanding consumer culture has produced the consuming self as the principal conduit of expanded consumer sales. In the market place of seekers, Roof identifies five major subcultures: dogmatists (for example, fundamentalists and neo-traditionalists) mainstream believers, born-again Christians (including evangelicals, Pentecostalists and Charismatics), metaphysical believers and seekers, and secularists. While Americans may invest less time in voluntary associations and are less certain about traditional Christian values than previous generations, they are significantly involved in spiritual searching that has produced a deeper emphasis on self-understanding and self-reflexivity. As the baby boomers came to maturity, they moved out of the narcissistic culture of the 1960s into a deeper, more serious "quest culture." If traditional religious cultures depended heavily on the continuity of the family as an agency of socialization, the transformation of family life and the entry of women into the formal labor market have radically destabilized religious identities and cultures.

These ideas about religious markets, demand for religious services, and consumption of religious phenomena are influenced by rational choice theory as an approach to modern spirituality. The paradigm has two interesting substantive claims. Rodney Stark and Roger Finke argued in *Acts of Faith* (2000) and *The Churching of America 1776-1990* (1992) that the religious demand for meaning is more or less constant across time—that is, wants remain more or less static. Hence, variations in religious behavior are influenced by supply rather than demand. Religious pluralism in America, by offering innumerable outlets for religious taste, promotes greater involvement. The theory, therefore, makes a useful distinction between demand for and supply of religious products. The paradigm effectively explains the proliferation of religious groups in the United States, the switching between denominations by customers, the inflationary character of the market, and the resulting hybridization and experimentation that is characteristic of modern religiosity. Of course, these religious markets are also global, because commodities and beliefs can travel rapidly. These markets cannot be controlled by religious authorities. While sociologists have (for good reason) become obsessed by religious fundamentalism, popular religion also flourishes alongside and in competition with fundamentalist faith and practice. However, fundamentalism succeeds because of their strictness that is by the very demands they make on people. Iannaccone's argument (1994) is that religions of high-demand, such as Jehovah's Witnesses, aim to avoid the free-rider problem by monopolizing the commitment of their followers.

Finally, the new model raises important questions about the elitist assumptions in such dichotomies as official and popular religion, the great and little tradition, or virtuoso and mass religion that have been common in "old" European theories. It is important to consider the word "religion," which has two distinctive roots (Benveniste, 1973). First, *relegere* means to bring together, or to harvest. Second, *religare* means to tie or to bind together. The first root points to the religious foundations of any social group that is brought together, and the second meaning indicates the disciplines or morality that are necessary for controlling human beings and creating. The first meaning includes the role of the cult in forming human membership, while the second includes the regulatory practices of religion in the discipline of passions. This distinction formed the basis of Kant's philosophical analysis of religion and morality. In *Religion within the Boundaries of Mere Reason*, Kant (1960) distinguished between religion as cult, which seeks favors from God through prayer and offerings. This type of religion brings healing and wealth to its followers. By contrast, religion as moral action commands human beings to change their earthly behavior in order to lead a better moral life. Religion can either refer to practices that bring good luck or to practices that cultivate human beings within a moral framework. The first form includes prosperity cults; the second, Kantian morals and Protestant discipline. In a hierarchical society where only the elite are literate, moralizing religions dominate popular practices. In a consumer society, the intellectual authority of ascetic religion declines and cannot adequately resist the impact of the new commercialized religions of wealth and health.

Differentiation of the Religious Market

We can argue that the globalization of religion takes three forms (Cox, 2003). There is a global revivalism that often retains some notion of and commitment to institutionalized religion (whether it is a church, a mosque, a temple, or a monastery) and an emphasis on orthodox beliefs that are imposed authoritatively. Within revivalism, there are conventional forms of fundamentalism, but also there are the Pentecostal and charismatic churches. Secondly, there is the continuity of various forms of traditional religion that are practiced predominantly by the poorly educated who seek healing, comfort, and riches from such traditional religious practices. Finally, there is also the spread of new spiritualities that are heterodox, urban, commercialized forms of religiosity that typically exist outside the conventional churches. These religious developments are no longer local popular cults, but burgeoning global popular religions carried by the Internet, movies, rock music, popular TV shows, and "pulp fiction." These can also be referred to as "pick 'n' mix" religions because their adherents borrow promiscuously from a great variety of religious beliefs and practices. These forms of spirituality are not limited to the United States or to Christianity. Films such as *Crouching Tiger, Hidden Dragon,* and *House of Flying Daggers* borrow from popular Taoist themes and this development is one aspect of "a new techno-mysticism most spectacularly presented to us in the use of special effects in blockbuster films" (Warde, 2006: 18). These phenomena have been regarded as aspects of "new religious movements" (Beckford, 2003) that are, as we have seen, manifestations of the new spiritual market places. Such forms of religion tend to be highly individualistic, they are unorthodox in the sense that they follow no official creed, they are characterized by their syncretism, and they have little or no connection with institutions such as churches, mosques, or temples. They are post-institutional and in this sense they can be legitimately called "post-modern" religions (Hunt, 2005). If global fundamentalism involves modernization, the global post-institutional religions may be regarded as typical of "post-modernization."

Globalization, thus, involves the spread of personal spirituality, on the one hand, and fundamentalist religion, on the other. Spiritualities typically provide not so much guidance in the everyday world, but subjective, personalized meaning. Such religious phenomena are often combined with therapeutic or healing services or the promise of personal enhancement through meditation. Fundamentalist norms of personal discipline appeal most to social groups that are upwardly socially mobile, such as the lower-middle class, newly educated couples. Spirituality is more closely associated with middle-class singles that have been thoroughly influenced by Western consumer values.

Religions in the modern world have been profoundly influenced by modern communication technologies. New media technologies can have contradictory effects, but they provide alternative, deregulated, devolved, and local opportunities for debate and discussion, and hence they make an indispensable contribution to a democratic civil society. The new media are important politically and sociologically because they have the unintended effect of corroding traditional forms of authority that are based on oral transmission or on print-based forms of textual learning that is linear, hierarchical, and repetitive. Knowledge based on oral transmission and memory, on the one hand, and print-based knowledge, on the other, are associated with traditional forms of authority and certain pedagogical technologies that produce a disciplinary self. At present, it is ironically unclear what disciplinary regimes, if any, are required in a knowledge society.

The God of the Abrahamic religions disclosed Himself, not through rational discussion, but through revelation—the carriers of which were the charismatic figures Moses, Jesus, and Mohammed. However, in a post-prophetic time, revelation can be approached routinely by human beings through the written word—the Hebrew Bible, the New Testament, and the Qur'an—and increasingly through religious websites that offer advice and free-flowing interpretation. With what Weber called the routinization of charisma, these religious cultures of the Book required scribes and scholars who interpreted the Word and passed on knowledge through repetitive forms of learning. Before the invention of printing, memorizing these revelations was an essential requirement of the survival of a religious community, and recitation was proof of piety. Traditional

Islamic learning is a classic illustration of a print-based religious culture that has promoted oral transmission through a discipleship relation with elders and religious teachers. Their traditional elites required specialized hermeneutics as the basis for their authority of interpretation. The Qur'an, which was according to tradition originally written down on the shoulder blades of camels, now is available in a multimedia environment. The Mosaic code, which was according to tradition originally written on tablets of stone, now is available in the story line of innumerable Hollywood films. Children grow up in a learning environment in which multimedia techniques are taken for granted. Educational programs for Muslim children regularly use animation to present Islam in a modern context. Insofar as we now live in a culture of print-based cultures, biblical cultures have to compete with or compromise with the new medium of knowledge.

A new brand of Christianity has emerged, particularly in America that is based on TV evangelism and the commodification of the Christian message; fundamentalist Islam has also been assisted by the use of cassettes to record and transmit the sermons of radical clerics. The recent death of Pope John Paul reminded us that he was the first media pope who fully recognized the power of the media in shaping attitudes and beliefs. Interestingly, the pope employed much of the media paraphernalia of a TV celebrity including the famous "pope mobile." Although modern fundamentalism benefits considerably from the global communication media, there are important differences between a world constructed on print-based knowledge and learning and a social environment in which texting is probably the most important means of communication for young people.

Conclusion: Globalization and Religion

In a famous article on "religious evolution" in the *American Sociological Review* in 1964, Robert Bellah developed an influential model of religious change from primitive, archaic, historic, early modern to modern religion. The principal characteristics of religion in modern society are its individualism, the decline in the authority of traditional institutions (church and priesthood) and awareness that religious symbols are constructs. Bellah's predictions about modernity have been clearly fulfilled in the growth of popular, de-institutionalized, commercialized, and largely post-Christian religions.

We can summarize the contemporary religious market by modifying the model of Harvey Cox (2003) in terms of a differentiation around four fields. First, there is simply the field of traditional institutionalized religions—Christian churches, synagogues, mosques, and temples with their formal leadership. These churches have elderly congregations, declining numbers, and shrinking budgets. Secondly, alongside this institutionalized field, there is traditional or popular religion that is localized, rural, and pre-consumerist. These forms of traditional religion exist at the village level and include folk religions that are aimed at healing and divination. These forms of religion are likely to decline with the spread of urbanism, education, and geographical mobility with migration. However, this is not always the case. For example, the sale of Buddhist amulets over the Internet is an illustration of how traditional folk practices can survive in a commercial and global context. These two fields, to some extent, correspond to the classical division between the "great and little traditions" that have been the subject of anthropological research for decades. Thirdly, there is classical fundamentalism that operates partly within the institutionalized field but more significantly outside it. These movements are essentially reformist and draw on the upwardly mobile lower middle and middle classes. These groups are the beneficiaries of post-war global educational growth in higher education. Fundamentalist and revivalist movements are often heavily influenced by consumerism in the form of the mega-church. Within these revivalist movements, we should probably differentiate between the charismatic movements—Pentecostalism and genuine fundamentalism. The former is heterodox and encourages speaking in tongues and other individualistic manifestations of possession by sacred powers, whereas mainstream fundamentalism is concerned to revive what it sees to be an orthodox set of beliefs and practices against the corruption of the present age. Fourthly, there is a global religion or new spiritualities that have often been regarded as the emergence of a new spirituality that is individualistic, heterogeneous, and that caters to urban youth groups who are the carriers of modern consumerism. This type of spirituality resembles modern consumerism—it is a "pick 'n' mix" religiosity that selects from a smorgasbord of concepts and practices. Madonna is perhaps the epitome of such religious consciousness.

Various religious goods and services are available in this market, but it is useful to recognize that the market is offering religious lifestyle as consumption. Just as we now have secular lifestyle clinics offering advice about household design, self-development, image, and presentation, so too we have (at least implicitly) religious lifestyle consultants. These groups are, in fact, selling piety and the consumer habitus. This is a market for religious services, but also a market for religious objects. Consumerism, for example, has an important impact in Islam around the market for *halal* products, that is, products that are deemed to be pure and consistent with a pious life style. To take one example, *classic Mecca Cola* is promoted in the Peninsular Malaysia and carries a certificate of authorization as *halal*. The company claims that 20 percent of profits are allocated to charity, thereby cementing the relationship between the consumer, orthodoxy, and the Islamic community or *umma*. This illustration further illustrates the underlying argument of this chapter, which is that we need to distinguish the relationship between religion and consumerism, on the one hand, from the idea of religion as consumerism, in which religious lifestyles are marketed through religious objects such as fashionable veiling, religious amulets, food, and drink.

These segments (fundamentalist, traditional, popular, and pious) of the global religious market compete with each other and overlap; the new spirituality is genuinely a consumerist religion, while fundamentalism appears to challenge consumer (Western) values, it is itself selling a lifestyle based on special diets, alternative education, health regimes, and mentalities. These segments have a degree of consumerism, but they are also distinctively different; gender is a crucial feature of the new consumerist religiosity where women increasingly dominate the new spiritualities; women will be, and to some extent already are, the "taste leaders" in the emergent global spiritual market place. While globalization theory tends to emphasize the triumph of modern fundamentalism (as a critique of traditional and popular religiosity) perhaps the real effect of globalization is the triumph of heterodox, commercial, hybrid popular religion over orthodox, authoritative, professional versions of the spiritual life. Their ideological effects cannot be controlled by religious authorities, and they have a greater impact than official messages. In Weber's terms, it is the triumph of mass over virtuoso religiosity.

The triumph of popular democratizing global culture is now having a deep impact on traditional hierarchical, masculine religions of the past. Turning finally to the title of this chapter, we can generalize by saying that in traditional society the dominant value emphasized the sacred: not goods, but gods. In early modernity with the rise of consumerism, the monopoly of orthodox Christianity was broken. We could summarize this by saying that the gods of consumerism competed with a traditional notion of divinity: not only God, but gods. In late modernity, there is an even more profound commodification of religion resulting in a new principle: gods can also be goods.

Consumerism now offers a paradise on earth involving both health and wealth. These tensions are probably most significant for the Abrahamic religions, but in this chapter I have concentrated heavily on Christianity. Because Jesus threw the money dealers out of the Temple, there is a strong theological message that condemns the quest for wealth, especially where it subordinates religion to material pursuits. In this discussion, we can see that the money dealers have returned to the Temple.

References

Adorno, T. (1991). *The Culture Industry*. London: Routledge.
Baudrillard, J. (1973). *The Mirror of Production*. St. Louis: Telos Press.
Baudrillard, J. (1988). *America*. London: Verso.
Beckford, J. (2003). *Social Theory and Religion*. Cambridge: Cambridge University Press.
Bell, D. (1976). *The Cultural Contradictions of Capitalism*. New York: Basic Books.
Bellah, R. N. (1964). "Religious evolution." *American Sociological Review,* 29: 358-374.
Benveniste, E. (1973). *Indo-European Language and Society*. London: Faber & Faber.
Berger, P. L. (1969). *The Social Reality of Religion*. London: Faber and Faber.

Bock, D. (2004). *Breaking the da Vinci Code*. Nasville: Nelson Books.

Bourdieu, P. (1984). *Distinction. A Social Critique of the Judgement of Taste*. London: Routledge & Kegan Paul.

Bruce, S. (1990). *Pray TV. Televangelism in America*. London and New York: Routledge.

Callewaert, S. (2006). "Bourdieu, critic of Foucault: the case of empirical social science against double-game philosophy." *Theory Culture & Society*, 23, (6): 73-98.

Campbell, C. (1987). *The Romantic Ethic and the Spirit of Modern Consumerism*. Oxford: Basil Blackwell.

Christ, C. (1998). *Rebirth of the Goddess*. London: Routledge.

Christ, C. (2003). *She Who Changes*. Houndsmill: Palgrave.

Crompton, R. (1996). "Consumption and class analysis," in Edgell, S., Hetherington, K. and Warde, A. (Eds) *Consumption Matters. The Production and Experience of Consumption* (pp. 113-134). Oxford: Blackwell.

Edmunds, J. and Turner, B.S. (2002a). "The distaste of taste: Bourdieu, cultural capital and the Australian postwar elite." *Journal of Consumer Culture*, 2, (2): 219-240.

Edmunds, J. and Turner, B.S. (Eds) (2002b). *Generational Consciousness, Narrative and Politics*. Lanham: Rowman & Littlefield.

Edmunds, J. and Turner, B.S. (2002c). *Generations Culture and Society*. Buckingham: Open University Press.

Finke, R. and Stark, R. (1992). *The Churching of America 1776-1990*. New Brunswick, NJ: Rutgers University Press.

Giggie, J. M. (2006). "The African-American holiness movement" *Society*, 44, (1): 50-59.

Hoggart, R. (1957). *The Uses of Literacy*. Harmondsworth: Penguin.

Hulsether, M.D. (2000). "Like a sermon: popular religion in Madonna videos" in B.D. Forbes and J. H. Mahan (Eds), *Religion and Popular Culture* (pp. 77-100). Berkeley: University of California Press.

Hunt, S. (2005). *Religion and Everyday Life. The New Sociology*. London: Routledge.

Iannaccone, L.R. (1994). "Why strict churches are strong." *American Journal of Sociology*, 99, (5): 1180-1211.

James, W. (1922). *The Varieties of Religious Experience. A Study of Human Nature*. New York: Longmans, Green and Co.

Kant, I. (1960). *Religion within the Boundaries of Mere Reason*. Cambridge: Cambridge University Press.

Kitiarsa, P. (Ed) (2007). *Religious Commodification in Asia. Marketing Gods*. London: Routledge.

Loader, C. and Alexander, J.C. (1985). "Max Weber on churches and sects in North America: an alternative path toward rationalization." *Sociological Theory*, 3, (1): 1-13.

Lukens-Bull, R. (2005). *A Peaceful Jihad. Negotiating Identity and Modernity in Muslim Java*. New York: Palgrave Macmillan.

Malthus, T. (1970). *Essay on the Principle of Population as it Affects the Future Improvement of Society*. Harmondsworth: Penguin.

Maresco, P. A. (2004). "Mel Gibson's *The Passion of the Christ*: market segmentation, mass marketing and promotion, and the Internet." *Journal of Religion and Popular Culture*, 8, (3): 1-10.

Mazower, M. (1998). *Dark Continent. Europe's Twentieth Century*. London: Penguin Books.

Meacham, S. (1977). *A Life Apart. The English Working Class 1890-1914*. London: Thames and Hudson.

Neuburg, P. (1972). *The Hero's Children: The Postwar Generation in Eastern Europe*. London.

Richards, T. (1991). *The Commodity Culture of Victorian England. Advertising and Spectacle 1851-1914*. London: Verso.

Roof, W.C. (1993). *A Generation of Seekers: The Spiritual Journeys of the Baby Boom Generation*. San Francisco: Harper.

Roof, W. C. (1999). *Spiritual Marketplace. Baby boomers and the Remaking of American Religion*. Princeton and Oxford: Princeton University Press.

Stanley, H. (1890). *In Darkest Africa, or the Quest, Rescue and Retreat of Emin Governor of Equatoria*. New York: Charles Scribners.

Stark, R. and Finke, R. (2000). *Acts of Faith. Explaining the Human Side of Religion*. Berkeley: University of California Press.

Tawney, R.H. (1926). *Religion and the Rise of Capitalism. A Historical Study*. London: John Murray.

Trentmann, F. (2006). "The modern genealogy of the consumer: meanings, identities and political synapses," in J. Brewer and F. Trentmann (eds), *Consuming Cultures, Global Perspectives. Historical Trajectories, Transnational Exchanges* (pp. 19-70). Oxford: Berg.

Turner, B. S. (2005). "The 1968 student revolts: The expressive revolution and generational politics," in A. Sica and S. Turner (eds), *The Disobedient Generation. Social Theorists in the Sixties* (pp. 272-284). Chicago: University of Chicago Press.

Turner, B. S. and Rojek, C. (2001). *Society & Culture. Principles of Scarcity and Solidarity*. London: Sage.

Vasquez, M. A. and Marquardt, M. F. (2003). *Globalizing the Sacred. Religion across the Americas*. New Brunswick, NJ: Rutgers University Press.

Veblen, T. (1994). *Theory of the Leisure Class*. New York :Penguin.

Warde, A. (1996). "Afterword: the future of the sociology of consumption" in Edgell,S., Hetherington, K., and Warde, A. (Eds), *Consumption Matters, The Production and Experience of Consumption* (pp. 302-312). Oxford: Blackwell.

Warner, M. (1981). *Joan of Arc. The Image of Female Heroism*. Berkeley: University of California Press.

Werbner, P. (1996). "The enigma of Christmas: symbolic violence, compliant subjects and the flow of English kinship," in Edgell, S., Hetherington, K., and Warde, A. (Eds), *Consumption Matters, The Production and Experience of Consumption* (pp. 135-162). Oxford: Blackwell.

Wuthnow, R. (2003). "The New Spiritual Freedom," in Dawson, L.L. (Ed), *Cults and New Religious Movements. A Reader* (pp. 89-111). Oxford: Blackwell.

Warner, R.S. (2004). "Enlisting Smelser's Theory of Ambivalence to Maintaining Progress in Sociology of Religion's New Paradigm," in J.C. Alexander, G. T. Marx, and C.L.Williams (Eds), *Self, Social Structure and Beliefs. Explorations in Sociology* (pp. 103-121). Berkeley: University of California Press.

Weber, M. (1966). *The Sociology of Religion*. London: Methuen.

Weber, M. (2002). *The Protestant Ethic and the Spirit of Capitalism*. London: Penguin.

Whyte, W. H. (1956). *The Organization Man*. New York: Simon & Schuster.

Williams, R. (1958). *Culture and Society 1780-1950*. London: Chatto & Windus.

Wilson, B. R. (1961). *Sects and Society*. London: Heinemann and California University Press.

Wilson, B. (1966). *Religion in Secular Society*. London: Weidenfeld & Nicholson.

Wolin, S.S. (2001). *Tocqueville between Two Worlds. The Meaning of a Political and Theoretical Life*. Princeton and Oxford: Princeton University Press.

Young, L. (Ed) (1997). *Rational Choice Theory and Religion*. New York: Routledge.

4

Dispossession: The Tenacity of Things[1]

David J. Ekerdt

The goal of this chapter is to map the problem of dispossession, that is, the parting of people and their things that occurs at the end of the consumption cycle. As opposed to a focus on expenditure and accumulation, dispossession is one topic among a set that might be encompassed by the concept of dis-consumption, others being such matters as saving (consumption deferred), taxation (consumption diverted to public purpose), or philanthropy (consumption transferred to others). Because dispossession follows upon possession and because possession entails durations of time, the retention and release of belongings is intertwined with the running of the life course. Possessions support growth, maturation, and the role trajectories of life. They do so in ways that may be historically specific to successive cohorts. Their disposal can also be an intergenerational matter. With an eye to age-related features of this topic, the present discussion will address people's motives for possession, occasions for dispossession, and the necessary labor of both.

In any consideration of the coincidence of people and objects, one tends to make a decision to follow one or the other. There is either a world of objects that encounter people, or a world of people sharing it with stuff. Object-centered thinking views things as having a life, a career, an arc, a death, a presence, an absence (e.g., Appadurai, 1986). As one follows the story of the thing, individual people come and go. Object-centered analyses are comfortable with production and consumption being all of a piece because production and consumption are sequential human acts upon the same thing.

Objects, as they are conveyed through time, are also seen to "call" for social relations: uniting people, discriminating among them, ritualizing their affairs. When disposed, or rubbished, objects may reappear to interact with humans in a new way (O'Brien, 1999).

The other route through this subject matter is people-centered, viewing things as occupants of people's attention, motives, behaviors, and thoughts. Individuals witness a flow of items through their worlds, often without regard to where objects came from and where they go upon being disposed of. The items themselves are secondary to their handlers. In considering the problem of dispossession, I am going to follow the people because person-object relations are central to the problem of disusing things. But theorizing is rarely so tidy, and it is not surprising to be traveling one axis of the intersection of people and things and then find oneself detoured down the other. For the parting of people and things, I also prefer the term *dispossession* rather than *disposal*. The two terms seem nearly synonymous, yet the latter connotes the materiality of objects whereas the former suggests a personal disengagement from things that is consistent with a people-centered analysis.

Why Possession?

Dispossession presumes possession, so having and keeping are matters that require preliminary attention. Not all the goods that a person acquires—by finding, buying, receiving, or creating—become possessions. Many items (e.g., food, cleaning products, newspapers) are used up in short order; experiences (a concert, a cruise) are had and, aside from any souvenirs, they are over. The consumer economy, it has been observed, grows ever more skilled at the provision of merchandise that flees possession—that needs frequent replacement. The lucrative possibilities of replacement consumption occurred early in life to the legendary American troubadour Woody Guthrie, himself not known as a partisan of capitalism (Brower and Guthrie, 2005). Guthrie started out as an itinerant artist, but soon realized that a customer would pay only once for a painting, but patrons could be sold a song performance over and over. From this insight was born a mighty career.

The popular impression of a disposable, throwaway society, however, needs some tempering. Does the acquisition of new domestic goods routinely mean that the old material is tossed out? Does the old flowerpot go to the rubbish, or is it stacked atop the other old flowerpots? "Out with the old and in with the new" may be goods specific. According to archeological evidence, the composition of flows to landfills over the twentieth century has changed to include a higher proportion of disposable packaging, food waste, and newspapers and magazines, but other categories of waste (e.g., textiles) have maintained a constant proportion (Lucas, 2002). This suggests that people don't readily toss everything, and that a culture of reuse continues in which the "replaced" possessions are perhaps stored, sold, or given away.

The items that become possessions are those that stay long enough to require the "labor" of possession. Kept things are far more than inert lumps of matter. What is kept must be placed, stored, arranged, contained, maintained, cleaned, insured, emotionally invested, and even "animated" in the sense that the possessor attributes to them an inner life. This living-with or living-into can be called cultivation, habituation, cathexis, appropriation, attachment, endowment, singularization, or decommodification (Dant, 1999; McCracken, 1988). Basically, I make the thing over as mine (Kleine and Baker, 2004). This is true to the root meaning of possession, which is based in the word "to sit"—the thing, as it were, settles in. Consumption, thus, often requires additional productive work to realize possession. To say that possessions are objects that are attended to and cared for does not necessarily mean that they are cherished; they could be merely tolerated, be resented, or even be hated. (It is also important to point out that possession is broader than "owning," which is a legal matter.) The essential point is that possession entrains labor on behalf of the things and their environs.

So, goods flow in and out of our lives but some objects stick and, so, we "have things." From here on, I am going to be more careful with language, preferring now the word *thing* over the word *object* when talking about possessions. Following the convention of "thing theory," objects are mere materiality, but things are those items invested with a subject-object relation (Brown, 2004). The stuff in your closet are objects; the stuff in my closet are things.

Things counted as possessions number far beyond the few items that are typically showcased in studies of possessions and their meaning, belongings such as antiques, curios, collections, and other cherished effects (Csikszentmihalyi and Rochberg-Halton, 1981). Rather, the totality of our things fill the buildings and rooms we live in, attics, garages, storage sheds, basements, automobiles, and gardens. We also keep possessions at our places of employment. You and I are shepherding a convoy of material that includes clothes, furniture, appliances, kitchen and dining utensils, tools, cars and their peripherals, photographs, heirlooms, records, documents, collections, decorations, seasonal displays, hobby materials, sporting goods, electronics, books, things that belong to others, food, plants, jewelry, cosmetics, toilet articles, medications, and pets. Like a Russian doll, possessions themselves contain possessions that contain possessions back to the deepest recesses of drawers and pantry cabinets.

These things are organized and categorized to various extents. One quality of the whole collection is that it reflects consumption according to age, period, and cohort influences. It is a tenet of aging and life-course studies that an individual's status, behavior, values, and identity are shaped by such influences. Accordingly, it follows that consumption should also be shaped by age, period, and cohort membership and that one's store of possessions should have these characteristics inscribed upon them. *Advancing age* lays down a residue of belongings acquired for successive roles, for bodily care, for self-development, and as gifts. Advancing age also furnishes the time durations within which things are cultivated or fall out of favor. *Period effects* on possessions come about when goods are historically new and enter households widely within a short span of time (e.g., forms of consumer electronics). Then there are goods acquired when a *cohort* enters the market for consumer goods at a certain historical moment. The things available at that time, such as books, recorded music, or furniture, can "date" the household if they are not later replaced with new fashions. In the aggregate level, cohorts of (aging) consumers are moving through the life course, replacing one another at various stages of life, thus layering the community with the material holdings from their unique historical experience. In all, the store of possessions, no less than the lives of their keepers, is the unique intersection of two dynamisms, individual aging, and historical change (Riley, Foner, and Waring, 1998).

Just to illustrate the density of possessions, I have a small bedside table with a shelf and two drawers. Its unruliness had begun to bother me, so I decided to declutter it and, in so doing, inventory its contents. It literally held hundreds of possessions, including books (20), magazines (21), pens and pencils (17), shoehorns (2), a pair of women's red leather gloves, a bag of old coins, and my father's medals from World War II. Some of these things I cannot imagine parting with, and some I cannot tell you why I have them or where they came from. In one drawer, a bottle of lotion had leaked and a number of things needed washing. Some items I relocated to other parts of the house. It took over two hours to review the lot and make selected decisions about their arrangement or disposition. However, most of the things eventually went right back into the drawers where they came from. The table is still unruly, but I am reconciled to its disorder.

The density of possessions also stymies research efforts to characterize household contents as a whole and even inquire about their collective meaning. How daunting would it be to inventory people's belongings? Gosling and colleagues (2005) have devised an instrument that can itemize and classify the objects in a space. Applying this technique to the dorm or sleeping rooms of college students, it took the research team the equivalent of one person hour to document the contents of each room. And these were only the *visible* objects, not those contained in drawers, wardrobes, or boxes, which would include, for example, multiple items of clothing or jewelry.

Why do we keep these things? The motives for possession (i.e., the ongoing commitment to the labor of possession—storing, cleaning, animating) are several. Our research on older people and their belongings (Ekerdt and Sergeant, 2006; Ekerdt, Sergeant, Dingel, and Bowen, 2004) has disclosed nine reasons to keep things. These will seem familiar because they are also reasons for acquisition, though the basis for acquisition may evolve into different reasons for retention. Shifting motives for possession are a given among observers of this behavior, leading object-centered studies to talk about things having "careers." It is also important to note that multiple motives can buttress the possession of a single thing (Kleine and Baker, 2004). And if one lives with others, there are items about the place whose possession is shared, or even mysterious.

As we see it, the nine reasons for keeping things are as follows.

1. *Things seem useful.* Everyday utility—now or to come—tops any list of possession motives, lay or scholarly. But things are instrumental to some end and so simple utility hardly exhausts the meaning of a thing. This is also the occasion to say that things have meaning not just in themselves but also in relation to one another. So, I have one shoehorn because it is occasionally useful, but why have I kept a second shoehorn?
2. *Things are worth money.* This possession motive is hypothetical pending an actual test of the exchange value of things in the marketplace.
3. *Things give pleasure.* All right, but "tastes" or "personal aesthetics" are a black box that begs for probing, for explanation, which is why the cherished-possession interview technique has been so productive for revealing people's attitudes and values.
4. *Things represent us.* They remind us who we are (material biography) and tell our story to others as signs, vehicles, and indicators (Belk, 1988).
5. *Things conjure the future.* Things promise possible futures and possible selves (Markus and Nurius, 1986). I will someday be the smart and learned person who has read the twenty books at my bedside or acted on their contents.
6. *Social reciprocity to gift givers.* Keeping things is keeping ties, a feature of the social order long observed by anthropologists (Mauss, 1990). The responsibility for doing this (Kleine, Kleine, and Allen, 1995) can make the household display of items more obligatory than aesthetic or sentimental.
7. *Responsibility to forbears.* This motive is most complex because family and ancestry are layered onto whatever utility, monetary value, or delight might already adhere to the thing. These are things that outlive people, durable and inalienable things whose disposal is unthinkable (Curasi, Price, and Arnould, 2004; Thompson, 1979).
8. *Conservation is a virtue.* This is a moral compulsion to retain things that are potentially useful to unspecified others. Remarkably, this motive endures in the United States whose citizens in 2006 nevertheless

generated 251 million tons of municipal solid waste, which comes to 4.6 pounds per person per day. My country annually trashes 9.1 million tons of furniture and furnishings, 8.6 million tons of clothing and footwear, and 1.1 million tons of books (U.S. Environmental Protection Agency, 2008).

9. *We keep because we can.* We dwell in ever larger containers, where the convenience of storage exceeds the inconvenience of disposition. The size of the American home has increased in the last thirty-five years from an average 1,500 square feet to 2,400 square feet. Is this house not big enough? The U.S. self-storage industry offers nearly 2 billion square feet of rentable space in 45,000 facilities nationwide (Dudley, 2007).

There has been some research suggesting that younger adults value possessions more for their usefulness, whereas older adults prize symbolic value (Csikszentmihalyi and Rochberg-Halton, 1981) but life-stage differences in the valuation of possessions are not well understood. There is also great conviction that the current generation of older people, having come through economic depression and war are frugal, waste nothing, and keep everything. A culture of scarcity has left them attached to their possessions and so inclined to retain things. The elders to come—the postwar cohort—grew up in an economy of relative abundance and so may more readily slough things off. But the next elders also grew up in larger houses in which retention was convenient. And, if material things have been relatively more important for the construction of identity, the Baby Boomers might have plenty of stuff left over from their lifestyle excursions. At any rate, there is at present no reliable technique for measuring multi-faceted possession attachment (in multiple possessions at that) and so speculation about cohort differences in possession rationales has yet to be tested (Kleine and Baker, 2004).

The list above of nine motives for possession could be subdivided into more or collapsed into fewer. The two most generic motives appear to be (1) instrumental control or effectance of one's environment and (2) the symbolization of self and others (Belk, 1988; Csikszentmihalyi and Rochberg-Halton, 1981; Furby, 1978; Richins, 1994). Sartre (1956) argued that that these two could even be collapsed into one; that *having* is essentially (a way of) *being* in the world. My father's war medals are me remembering; my sunglasses are me managing my comfort. Sartre's ontological insight, "I am what I have," is echoed through empirical research that repeatedly concludes that possessions are fundamental to a sense of identity (Dittmar, 1992). This immediately suggests that dispossession is going to entail more than the physical removal of material objects. Fromm (1976) posed the problem this way: "If I am what I have and what I have is lost, who then am I?"

Why Dispossession?

It next seems straightforward to predict that people will release a thing from their stores when all motives for its possession have been extinguished, in which case the labor of possession is not worth the effort. The thing is no longer valuable or delightful or carries the past. Alternatively, reasons for keeping may remain intact but the labor of possession becomes unsustainable—too costly in terms of time, money, or effort. So, possessions endure as such so long as motives for possession match or exceed the labor of possession. That is, motive $\geq$ labor. When the balance tips, the thing is a candidate for dismissal (Roster, 2001).

But it is only a candidate. The suddenly problematic status of not worth keeping may lead to a re-imagination of motive, i.e., the accentuation of yet another reason for keeping. I think that one could test the idea that possession motives #2 (worth money) and #8 (someone could use this) are the residual, last-resort rationales for hanging onto something that has lost all other purpose. I have long kept my late father's coin collection out of loyalty to his memory and an affirmation of our common boyhood occupation as newspaper carriers. But the coins' safekeeping gives me anxiety and I presently think that I keep them mainly for their value (which I plan to explore someday). Alternatively, the not-worth-keeping status could lead to the search for more possession resources—more space, help with maintenance, a lock box for those coins.

Next, pushing the question further, what might upset the relation [motive $\geq$ labor] and so set off the prospect of dispossession? I suggest three circumstances.

First, there are exogenous threats to possession that arise from natural and social sources. Things can rot, crumble, rust, wear down, or die, thus ruining their practical or emotional value. Things can be devastated by fire or smoke, violent breakage, water or mold, or vermin. Theft can remove possessions, and not only by burglary. We have met adult children who, believing that their parents have excess belongings, will take it upon themselves to trash things behind the elder's back. Items are also removed when possession is contested, for example, when property is divided during a divorce, or when goods enjoy familial ownership and another kin member claims a turn at possession. Dispossession by all of these exogenous means is involuntary and irretrievable. The things simply become functionally unavailable.

The second circumstance that puts possessions in doubt is some sort of failure with their capacity for social mediation. Goods, according to Douglas and Isherwood (1980), are the visible part of culture, vehicles of communication and membership. Yet they may someday fail to supply the information that we need for daily social commerce or the sentiment that sustains group or kin membership. We may find that they no longer represent our interests, identity, or rank, or they invite negative social judgments. We maintain clothing, utensils, machinery, furnishings, leisure goods, decorations, rooms, buildings, and yards. We may not have acquired all these things purely for purposes of strategic display, but display they do. They put our selves forward, presenting our persons as commodities to be regarded by others (Bauman, 2007). And if we sense that these things tell our story in an adverse way (e.g., we are out of fashion by some standard) it puts possession motives up for review. In my household, we have forsaken entertaining with our smallish, crystal wine glasses in favor of new flute- and globe-shaped stemware that is the current standard for serving white and red wine. Those old glasses—once wedding gifts—are no longer "us."

Social judgment about *excess* possessions—materialism—is the prompt for adults' periodic, voluntary campaigns at clutter reduction. The moral charge of "too much" is directed more at volume rather than specific objects. The downsizing imperative—a staple of popular media—has given rise to an entire industry that, hilariously, is another form of consumption. According to a recent news report, U.S. sales of home-organization products will rise to $7.6 billion by 2009. Closet-organizing systems are already a $3 billion-a-year business. There is even a National Association of Professional Organizers, 4,000 members strong (Green, 2006). The ability of capitalism to commodify anything, in this case dis-consumption, should never be doubted.

Life course change is the third circumstance inviting dispossession. Because we acquire and keep goods in order to fulfill social roles, it follows that role relinquishment might be the occasion to revisit possession motives. For example, work roles compel the acquisition of specialized clothing, tools, transportation, and self-care materials. Upon changing jobs, these materials may need to be refreshed. The successive stages of child rearing might lead to the relinquishment of goods and furnishings used to support infancy, then childhood, then youth. My home was once ankle deep in toys and playthings, of which only a residual few remain in a box in the closet, for visitors. Not only motives but also the labor of possession could come in for review due to role changes of the life course that divert time and money to other purposes.

Role change and moving on can leave some possessions not only functionally irrelevant but also negatively charged if former stages of life are now seen as undesirable. Disposition of belongings, though usually portrayed as a difficult process of detachment from self (Young and Wallendorf, 1989) can in some circumstances be a welcome occasion to push away possessions that are extensions of an undesired self (Lastovicka and Fernandez, 2005).

Concurrent with another kind of life course change, the labor of possession can become untenable with disability or with the normative narrowing of the life-world that occurs in later life. My colleagues and I have studied the particular instance of household disbandment when elders choose, or are forced to live in, smaller quarters where they cannot house all their things. Sometimes the downsizing is undertaken to anticipate life change, such as a move to care or even death. We know elders who have thinned their things in order to free adult children from any posthumous burden of excess possessions, or to protect their legacy from the judgment that they had had too much stuff. Though downsizing in later life appears as a surrender to age-related vulnerability, such "selection" of more manageable housing can be a positive, gratifying step (Marsiske et al., 1995).

Outplacement

The unbalanced relation [motive ≥ labor] is only the occasion for the dispossession of material. Next comes the act itself (Roster, 2001) and what might be called the labor of dispossession. The general term for this is disposal or, in its less latinate, more current version, "outplacement." The work of keeping is now weighed against the work of not keeping.

Our studies of older movers found a hierarchy of disposition strategies that people used during the short episodes of household disbandment. Of the possessions not intended for retention, people first made gifts of selected things. Then they attempted to sell other things, donating yet other things (some of which had been unsalable) and discarding another batch that had fallen into residual status. A single item might be subject to more than one disposal strategy. During this process, the meaning of things is tested and revised. These same strategies are available for any act or campaign of dispossession at any age, but not necessarily in the sequence that we observed during these intense downsizings. Gift giving is probably not a primary strategy among young and middle-aged adults. Given the secular trend toward larger dwellings, dispossession is likely to be voluntary until later life.

Gifts are fraught with calculation. The giver must imagine the appropriate possession relation [motive ≥ labor] in the receiver: that the receiver will find it useful, pleasing, or bonding to the giver; that the receiver can accommodate it or animate it (give it a "good home") as the possessor has. The timing of the transfer (the right occasion) must be planned, and there must be an eye to feelings of inequity among other potential recipients (Stum, 1999). The red leather gloves in my bedside table belonged to my late mother. They would be a perfect gift for my oldest daughter, but I have no comparable gift for my other daughter. So, for now, I continue to store the gloves. The significant risk in gift giving is that the receiver will not want the thing. If belongings that are invested with one's identity do not find heirs or interest among kin or friends, the failure to place them can be a source of grief (Marcoux, 2001; Marx, Solomon, and Miller, 2004).

A common reason for gift-rejection in intergenerational giving—older to younger—is that the recipient's household is already provisioned with the thing or that tastes in the thing are not mutually shared. For example, the possession of "fine things" such as china, silver service, and crystal glassware has been seen as the mark of domesticity among the current cohort of older women (Blaszcyk, 2000) but we hear now that the daughter generation does not welcome such "impractical" objects.

Sales to strangers are also a risk to the meaning that the possessor has invested in a belonging (Lastovicka and Fernandez, 2005; Price, Arnould and Curasi, 2000). The buyer's ability to undertake the labor of possession is not the seller's concern, but the seller's concept of the item's monetary value is about to be tested as the possession returns to being what it once was, a commodity in a marketplace. There is effort in getting the thing to market; it must be made presentable and then actually presented, even if only out to the street. Agents, such as antique dealers or online auction sites, can relieve some of the sale-related labor, but there is nevertheless effort (paying fees, acquiring know-how) in engaging these go-betweens. Interpersonal sales sometimes shade toward gift giving when the seller, sensing that the buyer's possession motives might be aligned with his or her own, cuts the price so as to guarantee the item's placement (Herrmann, 1997).

Donation—to community agencies, churches, veterans groups, arts organizations, libraries, museums, historical societies, humane societies—is also not without the labor of presentation and interaction with outside parties. In the US, such deposits are tax-deductible and so the goods' monetary value can be affirmed if only in a token way. Beyond convenience, donation has aspects akin to gift giving when owners place their things strategically to assure a continuity of appreciation and values, what Roster (2001) calls "safe passage."

Donation, as noted, can take effort and expense. Many an American household has bookshelves groaning with a hoard of golden yellow *National Geographic* magazines. What can be done with them? When an American soldier requested that people send their collections to children in Afghanistan, the response was generous. But some donors reportedly "backed off when they found that it would cost them $8 to send a box of 30 or so issues. Most opted to keep their magazines stockpiled" (Alcalá, 2007).

To *discard* might once have meant tipping things over the fence, down the ravine, or into the woods. No more. I can still burn things, bury them, and send them down the drain with minimal effort, but the rest of my trashing involves sorting and presenting (Hetherington, 2004). My municipal waste (limit: two bags per week) must exclude yard trimmings and leaves, recyclables, hazardous materials, and large bulky items. All of these categories have their own separate procedures for disposal, some of which I must contract out to others. If the rigmarole of rubbishing does not give one pause, then emotions may when facing the finality of disposal. Some people draw out the disposal process by placing doomed items in provisional exile at the margin of the household (e.g., the garage) later giving them final disposal when their ambivalence has been resolved (McCracken, 1988).

Even after possessions have left one's control, they may not be wholly gone, instead exerting an "absent presence" (Hetherington, 2004). As I have noted, people can continue to imagine the possible afterlife of things that they have given, sold, or donated away. Even with their garbage, they can perhaps take pleasure in thinking that recycling efforts have rescued items of trash for further use. The afterlife of gifts, however, does not need to be imagined; gifts can actually be visited to check whether the thing's new circumstances remain suitable. Perhaps this is why adult children refuse gifts from parents, because they do not want the responsibility of curating someone else's collection of stuff.

In summary, possessions are consumption items that stay long enough to merit some care, if only to be merely placed somewhere for later consideration. Across time, mixed and shifting motives for possession must match or exceed the labor of keeping them.

When the balance tips, there is still labor in the outplacement effort. Keeping or releasing, there is always work to do. The placing of things is the responsibility of consumption, and it sometimes seems a curse.

Things are tenacious—in the root meaning of that word, they "hold fast." Or seem to. It is we who are tenacious, because the bonds we create with our things are a "continuous creation" (Sartre, 1956) and those bonds are constitutive of identity. Dispossession, then, is nothing less than an encounter with our selves. Which is why downsizing and decluttering are not readily delegated to others—spouse, family members, appraiser, or the 4,000 members of the National Association of Professional Organizers—until the tenacious self allows.

Note

1.   This research was supported by grants from the National Institute on Aging, AG19978 and AG30477.

References

Alcalá, C. (2007, July 19). "Magazine's shelf life has no boundaries." *Sacramento Bee*: B1.

Appadurai, A. (1986). *The Social Life of Things.* New York: Cambridge University Press.

Bauman, Z. (2007). *Consuming Life.* Malden, MA: Polity Press.

Belk, R.W. (1988). "Possessions and the extended self." *Journal of Consumer Research, 15*: 139-168.

Blaszczyk, R.L. (2000). *Imagining Consumers: Design and Innovation from Wedgwood to Corning.* Baltimore, MD: Johns Hopkins University Press.

Brower, S., & Guthrie, N. (2005). *Woody Guthrie Artworks.* New York: Rizzoli.

Brown, B. (2004). "Thing theory," in B. Brown (Ed.), *Things.* Chicago: University of Chicago Press.

Csikszentmihalyi, M., & Rochberg-Halton, E. (1981). *The Meaning of Things: Domestic Symbols and the Self.* New York: Cambridge University Press.

Curasi, C.F., Price, L.L., & Arnould, E.J. (2004). "How individuals' cherished possessions become families' inalienable wealth." *Journal of Consumer Research, 31*: 609-622.

Dant, T. (1999). *Material Culture in the Social World: Values, Activities, Lifestyles.* Philadelphia: Open University Press.

Dittmar, H. (1992). *The Social Psychology of Material Possessions: To Have is to Be.* New York: St. Martin's Press.

Douglas, M., & Isherwood, B. (1980). *The world of goods.* New York: Basic Books.

Dudley, D. (2007, January-February). "Conquering clutter." *AARP Magazine*: 64-72.

Ekerdt, D.J. & Sergeant, J.F. (2006). "Family things: Attending the household disbandment of older adults." *Journal of Aging Studies, 20*: 193-205.

Ekerdt, D.J., Sergeant, J.F., Dingel, M., & Bowen, M.E. (2004). "Household disbandment in later life." *Journal of Gerontology: Social Sciences, 59B*: S265-273.

Fromm, E. (1976). *To Have or to Be?* New York: Harper & Row.

Furby, L. (1978). "Possession: Toward a theory of their meaning and function throughout the life cycle," in P.B. Baltes (Ed.), *Life-span development and behavior, Vol. 1* (pp. 297-336). New York: Academic Press.

Gosling, S.D., Craik, K.H., Martin, N.R., & Pryor, M.R. (2005). "The Personal Living Space Cue Inventory: An analysis and evaluation." *Environment and Behavior, 37*: 683-705.

Greene, P. (2006, December 21). "Saying yes to mess." *New York Times:* F1.

Herrmann, G. (1997). "Gift or commodity: What changes hands in the U.S. garage sale?" *American Ethnologist, 24*: 910-930.

Hetherington, K. (2004). "Second-handedness: Consumption, disposal and absent presence." *Environment and Planning D: Society and Space, 22*: 157-173.

Kleine, S.S., & Baker, S.M. (2004). "An integrative review of material possession attachment." *Academy of Marketing Science Review,* 2004, (1). Retrieved April 25, 2008 from http://www.amsreview.org/articles/kleine01-2004.pdf.

Kleine, S.S., Kleine, R.E., & Allen, C.T. (1995). "How is a possession 'me' or 'not me'? Characterizing types and an antecedent of material possession attachment." *Journal of Consumer Research, 22*: 327-343.

Lastovicka, J.L., & Fernandez, K.V. (2005). "Three paths to disposition: The movement of meaningful possessions to strangers." *Journal of Consumer Research, 31*: 813-823.

Lucas, G. (2002). "Disposability and dispossession in the twentieth century." *Journal of Material Culture, 7*: 5-22.

Marcoux, J-S. (2001). "The 'casser maison' ritual: Constructing the self by emptying the home." *Journal of Material Culture, 6*: 213-235.

Markus, H., & Nurius, P. (1986). "Possible selves." *American Psychologist, 41*: 954-969.

Marsiske, M., Lang, F.R., Baltes, P.B., & Baltes, M.M. (1995). "Selective optimization with compensation: Life-span perspectives on successful human development," in R.A. Dixon & L. Bäckman (Eds), *Compensating for psychological deficits and declines: Managing losses and promoting gains* (pp. 35-79). Mahway, NJ: Erlbaum.

Marx, J.I, Solomon, J.C., & Miller, Lee Q. (2004). "Gift wrapping ourselves: The final gift exchange." *Journal of Gerontology: Social Sciences, 59B*: S274-S280.

Mauss, M. (1990). *The Gift: The Form and Reason for Exchange in Archaic Societies.* New York: W.W. Norton.

McCracken, G. (1988). *Culture and Consumption: New Approaches to the Symbolic Character of Consumer Goods and Activities.* Bloomington, IN: University of Indiana Press.

O'Brien, M. (1999). "Rubbish-power: Towards a sociology of the rubbish society," in J. Hearn & S. Roseneil (Eds.), *Consuming Cultures: Power and Resistance.* New York: St. Martin's Press.

Price, L.L., Arnould, E.J., & Curasi, C.F. (2000). "Older consumers' disposition of special possessions." *Journal of Consumer Research, 27*: 179-201.

Richins, M.L. (1994). "Valuing things: The public and private meanings of possessions." *Journal of Consumer Research, 21*: 504-521.

Riley, MW, Foner, A., & Waring, J. (1988). "Sociology of age," in N.J. Smelser (Ed.), *Handbook of Sociology* (pp. 243-290). Newbury Park, CA: Sage.

Roster, C.A. (2001). "Letting go: The process and meaning of dispossession in the lives of consumers," in M.C. Gilley and J. Meyers-Levy (Eds.), *Advances in Consumer Research, Vol. 28* (pp. 425-430). Provo, UT: Association for Consumer Research.

Sartre, J. P. (1956). *Being and Nothingness* (H. Barnes, Trans.). New York: Washington Square Press.

Stum, M.S. (1999). "'I just want to be fair': Interpersonal justice in intergenerational transfers of non-titled property." *Family Relations, 48*: 159-166.

Thompson, M. (1979). *Rubbish Theory: The Creation and Destruction of Value.* New York: Oxford University Press.

U.S. Environmental Protection Agency. (2008). *Municipal solid waste in the United States. 2006 facts and figures.* Retrieved April 25, 2008 from http://www.epa.gov/garbage/mswpp.htm.

Young, M.M., & Wallendorf, M. (1989). "'Ashes to ashes, dust to dust': Conceptualizing consumer disposition of possessions," in T.L. Childers, R.P. Bagozzi, & J.P. Peter (Eds.), *Proceedings of the American Marketing Association Winter Educators Conference* (pp. 33-39). Chicago: American Marketing Association.

Part II

Historical Dimensions of Generation and Consumption

5

Old Age, Consumption, and Change over Time

Pat Thane

The everyday experience of most members of all age groups in Britain, including their patterns of consumption, has changed markedly over the past one hundred, even the past sixty and the past thirty years. Have the experiences of those defined as "old" changed more/less/differently from those not so defined? Does the concept of generation help us to understand change, or lack of it? Does the evidence exist to enable us to assess change over time in any meaningful way? Firstly, I will try to gather together the relevant evidence for, mainly, the past century.

It is well known that the numbers of "old people," and their proportion in the population, has grown dramatically (see Table 5.1). In reality, this gives an inflated view of long-run change. Even in the late eighteenth century about 10 percent of the population were aged sixty or above. The proportion of older people was historically low in the nineteenth century due to unusually high birth rates. Nevertheless, the proportion of older people has grown to unprecedented levels. To a significant extent this is due to falling birth-rates, before World War Two and since the 1970s. Of course, there is the issue of whether being sixty or sixty-five has the same meaning, physiologically or culturally, as it did three hundred, one hundred, or fifty years ago (to which I will return). Also, people are living longer. The probability of a male forty-five-year-old reaching sixty-five grew from about 73 percent in 1900 to about 91 percent in 1980; that of a sixty-five-year-old reaching eighty-five grew from about 18 percent to almost 60 percent over the same time period.[1] In 1950, a sixty-five-year-old woman could, on average, expect to live about fifteen years, a man about twelve years. By 2000, a woman could expect to live about another twenty-two years, a man about eighteen years.[2]

Table 5.1
Percent of Population Aged Sixty-Five and Over, Great Britain
1881-2001

Census year	Percent
1881	4.6
1911	5.2
1931	7.4
1951	10.9
1971	13.2
1981	15.1
1991	15.7
2001	18.0

Source: censuses

Equally important, the number living to be "very old" has also grown (see Table 5.2).

Table 5.2
The Very Old as a Percentage of the Elderly* in the UK

Year	Percent who are 75+
1901	21
1951	26
1977	30
2001	38

*males over 65, females over 60

Source: censuses

One hundred years ago about seventy people a year lived to their hundredth birthday. There are now 11,000 centenarians in Britain.

Most are female, since women continue, as they seem always to have done, to outlive men. Again, of course, the meaning and experience of being seventy-five, or eighty-five, or one hundred may have changed over time.

The best evidence also indicates that not only are more people living to later ages, they are remaining healthy and active to later ages—although older women tend to be less healthy than men, despite their longer life expectancy. The evidence for the improved health of older men and women is, as the Turner Commission on Pensions rightly stated, "frustratingly incomplete,"[3] since there is little systematic data going back more than twenty-five years and too much that exists depends on unreliable self-reporting. But, given the overall rise in living standards and in standards and availability of medical care especially since the World War Two, this is likely to be so.

Curiously, over the period in which healthy life expectancy has almost certainly been growing, the normal age of retirement from work has fallen. Those who could afford it have always ceased employment at the time of their choosing. The poorest always worked for as long as they were physically able, generally at increasingly degraded jobs. At the beginning of the twentieth century, retirement with a pension was rare. It was mandatory at the age of sixty in some departments of the civil service, in some other public sector and a very few private sector posts. The 1891, census recorded 65 percent of men as being in employment at age sixty-five. This fell to 56 percent in 1911. The fall is unlikely to have been influenced by the introduction of state pension in 1908 since this was not payable until age seventy and was so low, at 5 shillings per week maximum that it was unlikely, and was not intended, to encourage retirement from work. By 1931 the percentage of sixty-five-year-olds in employment had fallen to 47.5. This was a time of very high unemployment, when older unemployed men found it more difficult to return to employment than younger workers. Women also complained that they were likely to be pushed out of employment or found difficulty in gaining re-employment at still earlier ages than men, due to employer prejudice against post-menopausal women.[4] Also the numbers of occupational pensions, normally accompanied by retirement at sixty or sixty-five increased with the growth of white-collar employment between the wars, though they were not necessarily generous.

It was after World War Two that, gradually, retirement at or around the state pension age became normal for almost all British workers. Thirty-one percent of men were still in work at age sixty-five in the census of 1951, 23 percent in 1961, 19 percent in 1971, and 13 percent in 1980. Statistics for women are less reliable because much of the work carried out by older women before World War Two was casual and part-time work—cleaning, childcare, etc.—and unrecorded in the census, and after the war women's work patterns were still more irregular than those of men. In general, however, over this post-war period retirement as a phase of relatively relaxed life between paid employment and physical decline or death became an expected phase of the life cycle for almost everyone for the first time in history. The sudden transition from full-time work to full-time leisure was not always welcomed by the first generation of male manual workers to experience it. After long, hard working lives, often starting around age twelve or thirteen, in which the only long periods of "leisure" were likely to be stressful phases of unemployment or illness, the prospect of endless leisure was a shock for which they were unprepared. The transition to retirement was easier for women, even for those who had been in full-time work, since they were more likely to have maintained family and friendship ties outside the workplace; also the domestic side of their normal working day did not change. Later cohorts of men had time to anticipate and prepare for retirement. Why retirement spread so rapidly at this time is hard to explain. State pensions were somewhat more generous after the war than before, but they were hardly large enough to induce retirement at the minimum age. Most people experienced a serious drop in income on retirement. Peter Townsend, in his study of working-class families in East London in 1950s, described retirement as "a tragic event for many men, which has great repercussions on most aspects of their lives, not least their individual happiness and their security in home and family."[5] The men he interviewed had retired at ages as varied as forty-eight to eighty, mostly due to ill health.

He described their feelings of loss of status and independence on retirement and, not least, the loss of income. One man described how he no longer felt free to go down to the pub when he wished because he could no longer afford to buy a round. He felt that younger men felt obliged to buy for him, which, he believed, made him dependent even in his leisure time. His desire to consume had not abated, but his capacity to do so had been severely curtailed.[6]

Retirement at still earlier ages characterized the 1980s and 1990s as a feature of high unemployment and "downsizing" by businesses that preferred to shed more expensive, older workers. By the mid-1990s almost one-third of workers had retired by the age of sixty, some voluntarily on comfortable pensions, others not. By this time the bulk of retirees had had shorter and lighter working lives than those of the 1940s-1960s. Someone born c. 1930 would have left school at least at fifteen, while increasing numbers stayed on to sixteen or eighteen, and a higher proportion worked in less physically demanding white-collar employment than their predecessors. In recent years the trend to earlier ages of retirement has begun to go into reverse.

Post-war retirement was sometimes into a comfortable life, often not. Older people have, to varying degrees, shared the general rise in incomes and living standards over the past century and especially since World War Two. They have also shared the inequalities associated with class, gender, and ethnic origin of the rest of the population. The miserable, hopeless poverty experienced by many older, and also younger, people one hundred years ago has disappeared, but general living standards and also expectations have risen. This creates real issues of relative poverty and inequalities between socio-economic groups (including within generations). After narrowing between the late 1940s and the 1970s, they have since widened.

Everyone is now entitled to state pensions, as they were not one hundred years ago. State pensions were introduced in Britain in 1908, at first means-tested, but since 1946, universal. They have never provided enough to live on without supplement from some source. Means-tested state supplements of varying levels of adequacy have always existed, but a significant number of eligible people (currently 20 percent) fail to claim them. The Turner Commission found the UK pension system to be "among the least generous in the developed world." UK pensioners qualifying for the maximum state pension receive 37 percent of working life earnings, compared with at least 70 percent everywhere else in Western Europe.[7] About one-third of people above pension age currently live on incomes at or around the low level of basic state benefits. This is disproportionately true of women, long-term disabled people, and immigrants (due to shorter employment records; low earnings when in work; and, in the case of women, longevity and, increasingly, the effects of divorce) and all people over seventy-five. The remaining two-thirds of older people have at least adequate incomes for everyday needs and include a minority with relatively high incomes from occupational and private pensions and other sources. There have always been some very wealthy and some comfortably off older people. Their numbers have almost certainly grown over the past century, though firm statistics are hard to come by. They are concentrated disproportionately among white, married males aged under seventy-five.

Another important change in the twentieth century is that older people, by the end of the century, were more likely to have surviving children living within reach than ever before. The very high infant mortality rates of the whole of history before the mid-twentieth century, combined with the long European tradition of young people migrating in search of work, meant that in pre-industrial England only about one-third of people reaching their sixtieth birthday had a surviving child, and not all of those were close at hand. Possibly due to a realistic awareness that they might be on their own in later life, older people in England, for as far back as it can be traced, asserted a strong preference for independent living for as long as they were able. This was combined with an active contribution to their families (where they existed) and communities in the form of services (care for children and the sick, etc.) or financial when they could afford it. Better off older people long subsidized younger relatives or were donors to charity.[8]

Through most of the twentieth century birth rates fell, but most children survived and marriage and partnership rates rose so that by the end of the century, few older people did not have at least one child, though the strong preference for independent living in later life survived. Even when the generations did not live close together, modern technology—telephone, aircraft, motor travel, the internet—enabled rapid communication.

Overall, there have been major changes in the experience of later life and in the roles of older people in British society over the past century, as there have for all age groups. The number of people defined as "old" has grown in size and heterogeneity. One thing that has not changed is the cultural practice of defining "old age" as beginning around the ages of sixty or sixty-five, where they have stood throughout recorded history, despite real changes in the physical fitness of the average person in his or her sixties. "Old age" is thus defined as stretching from one's sixties to beyond one hundred. This group of "old people" includes some of the richest (such as Mick Jagger and Queen Elizabeth II) and the very poorest; fit, active marathon runners and some of the frailest people in society; and some of the most and the least educated. Older people are also increasingly culturally diverse as immigrants of the 1950s and 1960s grow older.

Clearly this large, extremely diverse body of people cannot easily be defined as a single social group, still less as a "generation." However, this has been recognized for many centuries. Even in late medieval England it was normal to distinguish between younger, or "green," old age when people were still fit and active, and the older, sadder, decrepit oldest age. The stages of life imagery that was popular from medieval times until at least the nineteenth century—visually representing men or women at seven, or ten, or twelve phases of life, from birth to death—conventionally depicted at least these two phases of old age and sometimes more. A French representation of twelve ages presented a steady progression of men and women from the "age of maturity" at age fifty—the pinnacle of the visual arc of the life course—to "declining age" at sixty, when the couple still look sprightly and alert; further decline at seventy, when they are a little stooped; at eighty they are "precarious," at ninety "decrepit," and at one hundred "imbecile." These were hardly representations of the life course of everyone, but it is improbable that such representations could have had such a long and widespread popularity had they been quite divorced from observable reality.

Concepts of "young," or "early" and "old," or "later" old age—or of the "third" and "fourth" ages—now normal in gerontology have a very long history. They fit uneasily with the concept of "generation" because the distinction between the younger and older phases of old age has always been, and remains, qualitative and functional rather than chronological. "Old" old age is often said, for convenience, to start around age seventy-five, but many people remain active long past that age. Those who survive to their nineties are often fitter and healthier than those twenty years younger [9] for reasons that are barely understood. Some people are frail in their sixties or even before.

That "old age" is partly a functional, partly a cultural construct, rather than simply a chronological one and has long been recognized in English and wider European discourse. Even the official rules in medieval Europe that fixed maximum ages for public service (e.g., on juries or in the army) usually at sixty or seventy, were applied flexibly recognizing the variable pace of human ageing.[10] For centuries people would first be addressed as "old," or so defined in official records, such as those of the Poor Law, at ages varying from their fifties to their eighties.[11] Records and images survive of very many active people of advanced ages through time.

Shakespeare's audiences clearly understood the diversity of the experience of ageing. Otherwise, it is hard to explain why Jaques' famous, miserable, depiction of the "seventh age" of man: "sans teeth, sans eyes, sans taste, sans everything"—often wrongly represented as a typical perception of old age at the time—is immediately subverted by the appearance on stage of the old retainer, Adam, who has earlier described himself as "at almost fourscore years," "strong and lusty." There are similar juxtapositions in Chaucer's works presented, as in Shakespeare, not as exceptional but as representations of normal life.

In the past, as now, differences among people of similar age have been at least as significant as differences among age groups. The very real differences in consumption patterns among older people, in the present and in the past, may be better understood in relation to physical capacity, income, gender, cultural background, and expectations (both of older people and about them by others) than to chronological generation.

Nevertheless, there are likely to have been changes over time in the patterns and tendencies in the complex range of activities we define as "consumption" by different age cohorts, whether or not we call them generations. The difficulty is to discern what they are, at least for any longer period than the past thirty years when data is more abundant. Hence, it is difficult to make robust comparisons over time or across and within age groups. Over the past century, and especially since the 1930s, objects of consumption have become more diverse and more of them accessible even to those on relatively low incomes, whatever their age, than ever before. It would be very surprising if many older, like younger, people have not experienced an expansion in the range and type of goods and services they consume. We should, however, remember past periods of rapid expansion of the world of material goods, notably the eighteenth century, an expansion which did not exclude even poorer older people. Peter King has shown how the eighteenth century consumer revolution penetrated even to the poorest and the very old of the population.[12]

Unfortunately, we have no systematic data over time particularly on the consumption patterns of moderately or very affluent older people, who have always existed as a substantial minority of the older age groups. Researchers on the lives of older people have generally focused on the poor because, understandably, they were mainly concerned about severe poverty and means to remedy it. Such research was mainly and increasingly a phenomenon of the past century. Due to the limitations of the research, there is a danger that in representing change over time, contemporary gerontologists may stereotype all older people in the past as living more limited, impoverished lives than younger people, forgetting the poverty of all age groups in the past. The pioneering major surveys of Charles Booth and Seebohm Rowntree at the turn of the last century concluded that the greatest cause of poverty was low pay, causing family poverty in all age groups. Rowntree, in his successive surveys of York (1902, c. 1936, 1950) described the social structure of the whole town but examined details of the income and expenditure only of working-class people. The survey by the Joseph Rowntree Village Trust in York in 1947-8 gained basic information on income, living arrangements, and other basic matters from all men over sixty-five and women over sixty living in York, 10,360 people. Their more detailed questionnaire, which captured more aspects of consumption, was administered to only about 60 percent of these (5996) selected because their health was seriously impeded, their accommodation was substandard, or their income below a certain threshold (i.e., the stereotypically "old.")[13] Similarly, the many "community studies" of the 1950s and 60s, such as Peter Townsend's *The Family Lives of Old People,* are enlightening about working-class lifestyles but rarely about the diverse age groups of the expanding middle class of the time.

In popular discourse, as in social research, people of later ages have often been perceived as "old" only when they fit a certain stereotype of dependency and apparent passivity. In the 1930s, for example, people in their sixties were deemed "too old" for work. No one apparently commented that Winston Churchill was "too old" to lead the country through a war when he reached the state pension age of sixty-five in 1939. All known cultures have prescribed "fitting" behavior, dress, etc. for older (and for younger) people and always some people, at least, have rebelled against the prescriptions.[14]

By contrast with the social research, the visual and documentary evidence over time is richer but unsystematic and it tends to be biased towards the better off. Images, diaries, letters, and other sources suggest that when older people have had the means, they have not been averse to consumption or necessarily very different in their consumption patterns from younger people, sometimes despite social pressures to the contrary. Certainly visual imagery does not show older people consistently using different dress codes from younger people whatever contemporary prescriptions may have attempted to lay down. Older men and women in the eighteenth century, and before and after, who tried too obviously to disguise their age by using the clothes and make-up of the young were ridiculed, but it does not seem to have stopped them.

Perhaps we can best interpret the changing consumption patterns of older people over the past century as sharing, as they always have, the expanding possibilities open to younger people. This is because more of them have rather higher incomes, better health, and more time and travel, cosmetics, and other items of consumption have become relatively less expensive. We should be wary of stereotyping older people at any time in the past as less active, more passive, consumers than younger people. Many have not shared these gains. Differences among older people continue to be as stark as those between them and people of other age groups.

Notes

1. Turner Commission, First Report, Appendices, p. 133.
2. Ibid., p. 3.
3. First Report, p. 28.
4. Dulcie M. Groves. "Women and Occupational pensions, 1870-1983," University of London, PhD. 1986.
5. P. Townsend. *The Family Life of Old People.* (London, 1957): p. 137.
6. Townsend, p. 152.
7. First Report, p. 58.
8. Pat Thane. *Old Age in English History.* (OUP, 2000): pp. 119-146, 287-307.
9. Kirkwood p. 210
10. Shulamith Shahar. *Growing Old in the Middle Ages.* (London, 1997): pp. 25-8. Thane. *Old Age.* pp. 24-7.
11. Thane. *Old Age.* pp. 26-7.
12. Peter King. "Pauper Inventories and the Material Lives of the Poor in the Eighteenth and Early Nineteenth Centuries," in T. Hitchcock, P. King, and P. Sharpe, *Chronicling Poverty. The Voices and Strategies of the English Poor, 1640-1840.* (London, 1997): pp. 155-191.
13. I am grateful to Mark Freeman, University of Glasgow, for this information.
14. Susannah Ottoway. *The Decline of Life. Old Age in Eighteenth Century England.* (CUP, 2004); Thane. *Old Age.*

6

Ageing, Cohorts, and Consumption: The British Experience 1968-2005

*Martin Hyde, Paul Higgs, Chris Gilleard, Christina Victor,
Dick Wiggins, and Ian Rees Jones*

Introduction

On the 15th of October 2007 Kathleen Casey-Kirschling retired. This ordinary event sparked an extraordinary reaction. Her
online application for social security benefits was attended by the
Secretary of State and broadcast across the American media (http://
abcnews.go.com). The reason for this level of interest is that Kathleen is officially recognized as the first American Baby Boomer.
And she is not alone. Over the next twenty years it is estimated
that she will be joined by a further 69 million of her co-boomers
(Kotlikoff and Burns, 2005). Nor is this an exclusively American
phenomenon. Although the baby booms in other countries, such
as Great Britain, France, and Finland, occurred a little later than
in the US, they too are all fast approaching retirement age. Interest
in and speculation about how the retirement of these cohorts will
affect government and society has emerged as one of the, if not
the, major policy and academic debates of the past decades (Lloyd-
Sherlock, 2002). However, these have principally focused on the
perceived economic impact that this will have in terms of increased
expenditure on healthcare and pensions. By contrast, relatively little
has been written about how this might impact on other aspects of
society and culture, such as education, tourism, or leisure pursuits.
An emerging area of interest is the possible relationship between
population ageing and consumerism.

These demographic trends raise a host of interesting questions about the nature (and sustainability) of present modes of consumption. Are older people outside of or excluded from consumer society? Do people buy fewer consumer products as they age? Are the baby boomers going to maintain their present levels of consumption after they have retired? Do different cohorts have different experiences and patterns of consumption in later life? In order to try to answer some of these questions it is necessary to outline some of the general features of population ageing and address some of the arguments regarding its impact. From there it will be possible to move to a description and discussion of trends in consumption and expenditure in later life in the UK over the past thirty years.

Boom or Bust?

Population ageing is global phenomenon (UN, 2002). The general trend toward longer life coupled with falling fertility rates throughout many parts of the world has resulted in greater proportions of older people in the population. On average, life expectancy increased by 9.2 years in the OECD from 1960 to 2002. However, some countries recorded much greater increases. For example, life expectancy in Japan rose by fourteen years, an average of one-third of a year per year, whilst in Turkey life expectancy rose by twenty years, an average of nearly one-half a year per year over this period. What is remarkable about these improvements is that, especially although not exclusively, in the advanced industrial economies they are due to gains in life expectancy from mid-life rather than those produced by combating infant mortality as was witnessed at the beginning of the last century (Manton and Vaupel, 1995; Vaupel, 1997).

As a result of these trends, it is estimated that by 2050 there will be almost 2 billion people aged sixty years and over throughout the world. If these predictions are correct then older persons will overtake the population of children, marking an unprecedented event in human history. These demographic trends are well publicized throughout Europe and North America. However, in the near future the largest number of older people is expected to be in the developing world. Today just over half of those aged over sixty years live in Asia, the largest numbers of which (some 130 million) are in China, and this is expected to rise to around two-thirds of the world's older population (Allen et al., 2002).

Whilst many celebrate this as an extraordinary achievement in combating many causes of premature mortality, many others believe that this heralds a series of radical challenges to the organization and function of present day society. Kotlikoff and Burns' (2005) dystopian view of 2030s America as "a country with large numbers of impoverished elderly citizens languishing in understaffed, over-crowded, substandard nursing homes" may be at the extreme end of this literature but captures many of the principal sentiments. There are two main areas of concern; labor market participation rates of older workers (often crudely referred to as dependency ratios) and projected healthcare expenditure. Labor force participation rates among the older workers have been falling drastically (Guillemard and Rein, 1993; Kohli and Rein, 1991; Yeandle, 2003; Laczko and Phillipson, 2004) and several national governments have already increased the statutory age of retirement and many others are considering similar policies as a consequence (OECD, 2007).

However, it is generally concern about future pressures on health-care that has generated the most alarm. Projections for the Wanless report in the UK estimate that there will be a 57 percent rise in the number of dependent older people between 2001 and 2031. Based on these figures, places in residential care facilities would need to expand by around 65 percent to 670,000 by 2031 and the number of home-care hours provided would have to increase to over 2.9 million per week by 2031, an increase of 48 percent. Overall this would correspond to a rise, in real terms, of around 148 percent in expenditure on long-term care, which would mean an increase from around £9.8b in 1996 to around £24.3b in 2031 (Wittenberg, Pickard, Comas-Herrera et al., 2001).

For many writers "the tidal wave of baby boomers that is mov-ing inexorably from changing diapers to wearing them . . . [their] numbers, their dilatory mating habits, their meagre rate of procre-ation, their romance with divorce, their plans to be retired *for as long as most people lived only a few centuries ago*, their prospect for an isolated, childless old age, and the protracted delay in their departure to the next world" are all to blame for this coming crisis (Kotlikoff and Burns, 2005, italics in original).

Changing Populations, Changing Societies

The idea that older people will represent a burden on state and society is being challenged (Gee and Gutman, 2000). Studies are revealing a picture of the present population of older people as healthier, wealthier, and more active than at any time in history. Contrary to the argument that increased life expectancy will come at the cost of an "expansion of morbidity" the "compression of morbidity" thesis holds that, even with increasingly longevity, the proportion of life that is spent in ill health, i.e,. with morbid conditions, will be concentrated to an ever shorter period prior to death (Fries, 1980; Fries, Green, and Levine, 1989; Fries, 2003). Evidence of declining rates of disability amongst older people from a number of American studies lends (partial) support for this thesis (Freedman, Crimmins, and Schoeni et al., 2004; Freedman, Martin, and Schoeni, 2002). Similar trends are evident from other studies in the UK (Bone, 1995), Italy (Minicuci and Noale, 2005), and the Caribbean (Reyes-Ortiz, Ostir, and Pelaez et al., 2006). Even when chronic illnesses, such as cardiovascular disease, are present they seem to be less disabling than they would have been in the past (Crimmins, 2004).

Throughout much of the advanced industrialized world, the economic position of older people has, along with that of the general population, improved markedly over the past few decades (Casey and Yamada, 2002). In the UK, income levels increased from the 1960s onwards (Atkinson, 2000) and many older people benefited from these increases both during their working lives and in retirement. As a consequence, levels of poverty in retirement have changed considerably. At the end of the 1970s, almost half of pensioner households in Britain were in the bottom income quintile before housing costs, but by 2005 this had dropped to around a quarter while the proportion of pensioner families in the middle-income quintile had gone from 13 to 21 percent (DWP, 2006).

These improvements in the health and financial circumstances of older people have prompted many writers to argue for a more positive (re)conceptualization of later life as an active and potentially productive time of life. Peter Laslett has been credited with doing much to promote these ideas, especially in the UK. Borrowing from the French notion of the *troisème age,* he argued for a new conception of later life as a "third age," free from the responsibilities of work and childrearing, whose occupants were able to engage in socially productive activities such as volunteering (Laslett, 1996). In the US, terms such as "productive ageing" (Bass and Caro, 2001) and "successful aging" (Rowe and Kahn, 1998) have emerged to express a very similar set of arguments. Although these ideas are not without their critics (Bury, 1995; Scheidt, Humphreys and Yorgason, 1999) they have proved to be a valuable corrective to the often myopic and negative stereotypes of older people.

These demographic changes have not occurred in a vacuum but have taken place alongside a series of (radical) transformations in society. These changes have been conceptualized variously as the shift from "organized" to "disorganized" capitalism (Lash and Urry, 1997), from Fordism to post-Fordism (Amin, 1997), or from a high or first modernity to a late or second modernity (Giddens, 1991; Beck, Bonss and Lau, 2003). However all denote a rupture between a previous, more determinate set of social processes and the present, fluid, indeterminate, and ambiguous modes of living.

The effects of these changes are evident if one considers the recent history of the UK. In pre-war, 1930s Britain, peoples' lives conformed to a regular or institutionalized pattern with comparatively short spells of education before a long period of full-time work, marriage, and childrearing, culminating in a short period of retirement (Warnes, 2006). However, the considerable economic and social changes that emerged following the war resulted in a number of challenges to this "normalized life course." By the end of the twentieth century, the life course had become more unstable, less constrained by the institutional frameworks of education, work, and family (which themselves had changed) coupled with longer life expectancy and earlier retirement ages. The emergence of new life courses, changes in the social structure, increasing individualization, and familial dynamics have been linked by some to increasing inequalities in later life (Irwin, 1999) as well as being viewed as opening up new possibilities for later life (Gilleard and Higgs, 2000). This de-standardization of the modern life course has been hailed by a number of social theorists as a key feature of "second" modernity (Bauman, 1995; Castells, 1996; Kohli and Meyer, 1986).

Later Life in Second Modernity

Second modernity refers to "the modernization of modern society" in which older, modern institutions and structures are transformed (Giddens, 1991; Beck, Bonss, and Lau, 2003). A key development in this shift has been the privileging of consumption over production as the principle site for the construction of identity. Although there is a small, but growing, body of work on the (inter-)relationships between population ageing and globalization (Polivka, 2001; Wilson, 2002) and post-Fordism (Jackson, 2006; Taylor-Gooby, 2002; Pierson, 2001) relatively little has been written on consumption and later life (Gilleard and Higgs, 2000). Given the historical co-incidence (some might even argue contingency) of these demographic and social changes as well as the fundamental interconnectivity between age structures and social structures (Gordon and Longino, 2000) it ought to be problematic, if not impossible, to understand the experience of later life today without reference to the rise of mass consumer society.

What we recognize today as consumer society has complex historical roots (Sassatelli, 2007) based, as it is, on the wide diffusion of commodities, goods, objects, and luxury items that grew in volume and range from the seventeenth century onwards. In the context of second modernity, it has become increasingly based on commoditization at a global scale and the proliferation and replication of styles and tastes in mass markets. Historical studies of consumption have shown that consumer and material culture predate industrialization (Fairchilds, 1998; Trentman, 2004). Stearns (1997) argues that consumer society developed from an early modern phase spanning the seventeenth and eighteenth centuries, a second stage of consumer growth in the late and early nineteenth centuries, and a third phase of mass consumerism reaching maturation in the twentieth century. The earlier stages of consumerism and material culture were largely based on goods produced in small, flexible units with specialized distribution methods rather than the massive standardized firms and complex trans-national distribution networks that characterize the post-war era. However, following the end of World War Two, the range and number of consumer products available to mass markets increased at a breathtaking pace (Oldenziel, de la Bruhèze, and de Wit, 2005) and as these markets matured, distribution systems became more efficient and the goods became cheaper and key items became increasingly available and affordable. The phasing of these developments has varied in different countries (Strausser, McGovern, and Judt, 1998) but, by the beginning of the twenty-first century, the global economy has become dominated by the imperatives of mass consumption.

It is important to recognize that people at or reaching retirement age today participated in the rise of these mass-consumer markets. In British society, for example, there is growing evidence of the increasing material and symbolic participation of older people in modern life. Analysis of consumption trends in the UK in the last quarter of the twentieth century indicates a dramatic fall in the proportion of household expenditure spent on food, clothing, and fuel and a sharp rise in spending on cars, holidays, and eating out. Over the same period, households have experienced a growth in non-housing expenditure. It is of some significance that after equivalizing for household size, the households experiencing the largest growth in household spending have been those of couples with children, elderly couples, and young couples without children (Blow, Leicester, Oldfield, 2004).

Visions of the third age that emphasize its distinctive lifestyle defined through the consumption and leisure patterns, "silver surfers," "woopies," or "new agers" have begun to emerge (Gunter, 1998). Although these ideas are largely the province of market researchers and economists seeking to draw attention to the wealth and spending habits of retired people (Smith and Clurman, 1997) a few sociologists and social gerontologists are beginning to engage with these trends.

Gilleard and Higgs (2000; 2005) have argued that standard accounts of ageing identities based on a socialized life course with clear demarcations between adult and late adult life are already inadequate. Previous certainties about post-working life (retirement, disengagement, and old age) are disappearing, replaced by a variety of diverse lifestyles sharing a freedom secured from lack, but also sharing new, uncertainties, anxieties, and aspirations. Central to this is their engagement with consumer lifestyles. Modernist binary thinking, which constructed an impoverished and devalued status of old age as the "other" to productive labor is no longer sustainable within a post-industrial, post-productivist culture. Older people are no longer a distinct group excluded from consumer society. Instead, they have become actively engaged sharing its opportunities and dangers along with other sections of society. Later life has, therefore, emerged as a new social field that has become more diffuse, heterogeneous, and multidimensional—and much of the concerns and anxieties about this have centered on the so-called baby boomer generation.

My Generation

The burgeoning literature on the baby boom has put the terms cohort and generation at the forefront of many academic and policy discourses (Turner, 1989; Becker, 1991; Gilleard and Higgs, 2000; Gilleard and Higgs, 2005). Yet, the idea that social change and demography are closely linked is far from new. Ryder saw cohorts as an "aggregate of individuals who experienced the same event within the same time interval" (Ryder, 1997: 68). The "effect" of this collective experience is deemed to be carried by a cohort throughout their lives (Hardy and Waite, 1997: 6). Anthropologists share a similar notion of the cohort as the victim and vehicle of social change. Foner (1984) argues that each age cohort is the "product of [the] changing social environment its members experience over the lifecourse . . . [and that it] bears the stamp of the historical context through which it flows."

Within political sociology, there has been a longstanding interest in "generational cohort analysis" (Cutler, 1977). Here the approach has been to draw boundaries around birth cohort groups and link these boundaries to putatively iconic "moments" in history which thus define the generation. Vincent (2005), for example, argued that the collective childhood experience of living through World War Two helped to create a "war generation" in Britain. Whittier (1997) argued that she was even able to identify "micro-cohorts" from within the Women's Movement in Ohio based on state of the movement, i.e., growth, stability, or decline, when each woman joined. Differences in political attitudes between these micro-cohorts were still detectable several decades after respondents had left the movement and the organization ceased to exist.

There are subtle but important conceptual differences between cohorts and generations. Whilst a cohort approach is largely quantitative, grouping individuals together on the basis of their year of birth, a generational approach involves a qualitative dimension; that the members of that generation have an awareness of themselves as a culturally distinct social body. Thus, Harrison White (1992) defines generation as "a joint interpretive construction which insists upon and builds among tangible cohorts defining a style recognized from outside as well as from inside itself."

In his seminal paper on the "problem of generation" Mannheim (1997) wrote that the term "generation" contained two related and essential elements. The first refers to a common location in historical time (generational location); the second to a distinct consciousness of that historical position, a "mentalité" or "entelechie" formed by the events and experiences of that time (generational style). Both location and consciousness are necessary elements, in Mannheim's formulation, in order that "generation" can function as a structuring process on a par with the vertical structures of class and gender. Although this formulation has been criticized for its conceptual imprecision (Ryder, 1984; Kertzer, 1983; Abrams, 1970), the Mannheimian concept of generation has persisted within the social sciences and offers a valuable approach to exploring changing patterns of consumption in later life.

Building on Mannheim's work, Gilleard and Higgs (2005) stress the distinction between "cohort" and "generation." They reject the view of a generation as a birth cohort whose identity is defined by exposure to a specific event or set of '"socializing" events. Instead, they argue, generations represent a distinct, temporally located cultural field within which individuals from a variety of overlapping birth cohorts participate as generational agents. By adapting Bourdieu's (1977) concepts of "habitus" and "field," generation becomes not so much an aggregate of individuals born at a certain time, but a cultural field emerging at a particular moment in history, distributed through a new mass culture (Gilleard and Higgs, 2005). Such a cultural field shapes and is shaped by the particular tastes, values, and dispositions of those cohorts whose interpretations of the world have been most influenced by mass culture. This allows Mannheim's concept of a generational location to be redefined as a generational "field," characterized by the emergence of a changed relationship between past and present social spaces. Generational style or consciousness is treated, in like fashion, as a generational "habitus"—a set of dispositions that generate and structure individual practices that emerge and are defined by the forces operating within a particular generational field.

Gilleard and Higgs (2005) argue that there are three advantages of formulating "the problem of generation" in this way. First, it avoids the problem of a conflation between age groups, cohorts, and periods, whereby each is defined as the product of the other two. As has been pointed out by many earlier writers, because each of these terms is treated as being constituted out of the other two, no distinct explanations can be made for one element without it being equally determinate for the others (Palmore, 1978). Treating generation as a cultural field avoids defining it by reference to the membership of a specific cohort. Second, such an approach enables actors to be treated as individuals who will inevitably vary in their level of engagement with emerging and established generational fields. Each individual member of a birth cohort need not serve as a "representative" of this or that generation but the generational field is defined through the pattern of linkages between different lifestyle practices. Third, this approach recognizes the importance of changing material conditions that structure the symbolic exchange that mediates such patterns of engagement, enabling a focus upon the motors that drive the new circuits of cultural capital.

The foregoing arguments set up an interesting and important question: are the baby boomers driving a new, consumerist, experience of later life or did the sixties generation create a new generational habitus that has spread out, albeit unevenly, to encompass other age groups radically transforming later life for all? Put more prosaically, is the changing nature of later life a product of crude demography or due to a historically located change in the nature of capitalism? Thus, it is possible to identify two closely related but competing theories for the rise in consumer lifestyles amongst older people today: a *"cohort hypothesis,"* that the demographic weight of the baby boom created the necessary conditions for a mass consumer society and that this cohort is the vanguard of this consumer culture, and a *"generational hypothesis,"* that changes in the organization of capitalism, during the 1960s, has created a consumer society that, despite its initial emergence amongst youth culture, has colonized all age-strata and that this transformation of later life would have occurred with or without the baby boom.

The purpose of this chapter is, thus, twofold: to chart the patterns of expenditure and ownership of goods amongst British retirees and to (tentatively) explore the relationships between ageing, cohort, and consumption within this context.

Methods and Data

The Study

In the UK, as elsewhere, there are an increasing number of longitudinal studies that should allow researchers to explore the dynamics of individual and cohort ageing in the near future. However, at present these are either too recent, such as the English Longitudinal Study of Ageing (ELSA), or have too few participants who are old enough, such as the 1958 MRC birth cohort, to yield sufficient information to look at the consumption and lifestyle experiences of different cohorts over a long enough period of time.

However, data on expenditure patterns in the UK has been collected annually by the government since the 1950s through the Family Expenditure Survey/Expenditure on Food Survey (FES/EFS). The FES/EFS is a voluntary survey of a random sample of private households in the UK carried out by the Office for National Statistics (ONS). The FES/EFS is primarily a survey of household expenditure on goods and services. However, it contains a wealth of other data on the household and its members, such as age, sex, income, and labor-market status.

The original purpose of the survey was to provide information on spending patterns for the purpose of calculating the Retail Price Index (RPI). The survey has been conducted annually since 1957 although, since 1994, the survey reference period has changed from the calendar year to the financial year. Data collection is carried out throughout the year to avoid potential bias arising from seasonal variations in expenditures. The basic unit of the survey is the household although data is collected on both the household and the individual level.

The FES/EFS sample for Great Britain is drawn from the Small Users file of the Postcode Address File. From this 672 postal sectors in Great Britain are randomly selected during the year after being arranged in strata defined by Government Office regions (sub-divided into metropolitan and non-metropolitan areas) and two 1991 Census variables—socio-economic group and ownership of cars. On average about seven thousand households are included and surveyed each year representing an average response rate of 60 percent, although this has declined over the period covered in this chapter.

Rather than use data from each year, it was decided to take a sample of nine years of the FES/EFS at roughly five-year intervals over the period from 1968 to 2004/5. These data were accessed through the Economic and Social Data Service (ESDS). By using a repeat cross-sectional design, it is possible to construct a number of time series, from these data, on the expenditure and ownership of certain goods from the late 1960's to the present day.

Ownership of Consumer Durables

At each year, the FES/EFS collected information about a range of goods owned by the household. For the purpose of these analyses goods were selected that were common to as many years as possible in order to explore changes over time. Household ownership of a telephone was recorded in each of the data years. Television ownership was asked in all years apart from 1993. However, in 1988 the question changed to how many televisions the household had, from simply whether the household owned a television. To maintain comparability over the time period, the responses in these latter waves were recoded into whether the household owned at least one television against households where there was no television. Whether the household owned a washing machine and whether the household owned a car were tabulated each year from 1973 to 2004/5. We were also keen to find out about the ownership of new consumer goods resulting from technological advance. Given their more recent development, these variables were available for a much shorter time span and consequently had trajectories that were much more truncated. From 1993, respondents were asked whether the household owned a video cassette recorder (VCR), a personal computer (PC), or a microwave oven.

These goods were grouped into two broad classifications simply based on how long they have been on the market. Under the label "Established goods" were grouped phones, TVs, cars, washing machines, and fridge-freezers. "Novel goods" consisted of microwaves, dishwashers, VCRs, and PCs.

Expenditure Data

All members of the household were asked to maintain an expenditure diary over fourteen days, in which they were required to record details of everything they bought during that period. The range of items is comprehensive including everything from the banal, such as bread and milk, to expensive luxury items, such as motorboats. Respondents recorded not just the item that they bought and the cost, but how it was purchased (i.e., cash, credit card, or hire purchase) and, in the case of some food and drink items, whether it was consumed inside or outside the home. Expenditure data on individual items (although interesting in themselves) are aggregated into a number of general categories. Categories that are common to as many data points as possible were chosen to give the most comprehensive picture possible. These were expenditure on (1) food, (2) fuel, (3) travel and transport, (4) household goods, (5) tobacco, (6) alcohol, and (7) clothing.

However, as with the ownership data, the type and composition of these categories have changed over time. Some of these changes are merely nominal. For example, after 1988 expenditure on transport was sub-divided into expenditure on fares and expenditure on motoring. However, the individual items that made up these categories did not radically change and therefore it is possible to recombine them to give a continuous time series of expenditure on transport. Some changes reflect the fact that certain goods, such as coke (the derivative of coal rather than the soft drink) are no longer used, whilst others, such as mobile phones, have only relatively recently appeared. Where this is the case and items have been removed or added, the Office of National Statistics (ONS) categorizations have been taken to be socially and culturally meaningful, and, although not directly comparable, are assumed to be conceptually comparable over time.

Findings

Creating Cohorts/Generating Generations

Unlike a birth cohort, with its clear temporal boundaries, it would be extremely difficult, perhaps even impossible, to create an empirical measurement of a generational consciousness or habitus with the data in the FES/EFS. Nor is it possible to do a proper cohort analysis given the cross-sectional nature of the data. However, it is possible to create a series of pseudo-cohorts for each of the years for which we have data by allocating individuals each year to a particular birth cohort based on their year of birth. Based on the large random sample for each study, it is therefore assumed that members of these pseudo-cohorts are representative of the wider cohort and can be used to look at trends across time.

As noted above, finding an agreed upon definition of what constitutes a birth cohort, never mind a baby boom, is problematic. For example, some writers identify just one post war baby boom, those born between 1946 and 1965 (Huber and Skidmore, 2003) whilst others argue that there were in fact two booms, one from 1946 to 1954 and another from 1955 to 1965 (Biggs, Phillipson, and Leach et al., 2006) sometimes referred to as the "echo-boom" or "generation Jones." Cohorts can be variously defined by a certain set interval, such as ten-year birth cohorts, or by living through certain cohort-forming events, such as World War Two. However, both approaches are problematic either by fetishizing a certain temporal frame, such as the decade, or by focusing too much attention on certain events at the expense of others. Therefore, given the focus on demographic change, an empirical approach using the annual number of live births was adopted to define each cohort rather than a top-down approach, which imposes temporal boundaries, of say 5 or 10 years, onto history. Figure 6.1 shows the number of live births per annum in the UK from 1880 onwards and the demarcations for each of the cohorts. Different cohorts were classified on the basis of patterns in the birth rates. As a result not all cohorts are of equal size. However, it is felt that this approach best captures the demographic phenomena, the baby-booms, that are the focus of the chapter. The cohorts have been assigned labels based on their historical timing, such as the Depression babies. However, although there is often a good degree of coincidence between these events and the cohorts, it should not be assumed that they are based on or formed by these events. Moreover the labels should be seen as heuristic devices, employed to aid the reader rather than accurately reflect the exact dates of the events they refer to. This is clearly the case when looking at the "WW2 babies" cohort which starts in 1936 and ends in 1943. Although World War Two is generally seen to begin in 1939, with the German invasion of Poland, and end in 1945, with the surrender of both German and Japanese forces, it is felt that this has an intuitive appeal as a label for those born between these years.

For the purpose of these analyses, households were allocated into pseudo-cohorts based on the year of birth of the head of the household (HoH). In the FES, the head of the household is defined as follows: The HoH must be a member of the household and is, in order of precedence, the husband of the person or the person who either (a) owns the household accommodation, or (b) is legally responsible for the rent of the accommodation, or (c) has the household accommodation as an emolument or prerequisite, or (d) has the household accommodation by virtue of some relationship to the owner, lessee, etc. who is not, himself, a member of the household. In the case of a married couple, where both are

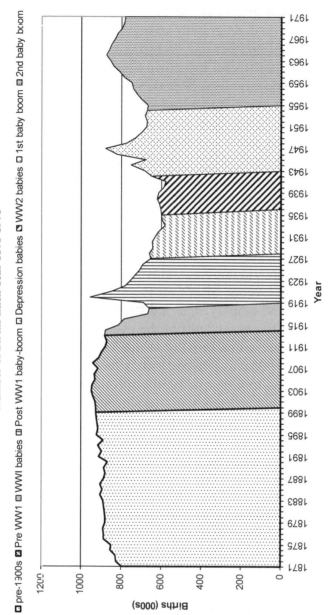

Figure 6.1
Number of Births Each Year 1871-1971

□ pre-1900s ⊠ Pre WW1 ▨ WWI babies ▦ Post WW1 baby-boom ▨ Depression babies ▨ WW2 babies □ 1st baby boom ▨ 2nd baby boom

Births (000s)

Year

Source: ONS; Historical series FM1 No 13

members of the household, the husband is the HoH, even if the wife owns the property. If the husband is not a member of the household, but the accommodation is in his name, his wife is the HoH. If two members of different sexes have equal claim the male is to be take as HoH. If two members of the same sex have equal claim, the older is taken as HoH.

Trends in Ownership and Expenditure in Later Life

Figure 6.2 shows the average age for each of the pseudo-cohorts for each of the FES/EFS surveys used in these analyses. Obviously different cohorts enter later life at different years. For example, if we use sixty years as a rough indicator of later life, the oldest two cohorts are already at or over this in 1968 whilst those born around the Depression only cross this threshold, on average, in 1993. Thus, although as mentioned above, it is not possible to track ownership and expenditure patterns across individual life courses it is possible to get some idea of age-associated consumption for different birth cohorts. If, as cohorts age rates of ownership or patterns of expenditure fall this would suggest age related decline within that cohort.

Figure 6.2
Mean Age of Pseudo-Cohort by Year

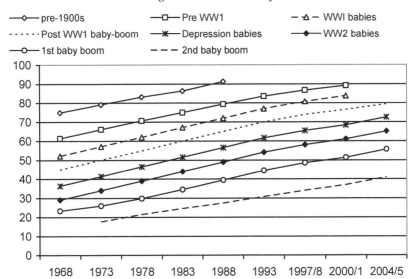

Turning first to the established goods, several different trends are evident. As Figure 6.3 shows, levels of phone ownership were relatively low for all cohorts in the late 1960s, the earliest point for which there is reliable data. However, it is the oldest (pre-1900) and the youngest (first baby boom) cohorts that have the lowest levels of ownership with only around one-fifth of households in these cohorts owning a phone. Rates of ownership in all cohorts rise steadily across the period even amongst the oldest cohort (although there ceases to be data available on them after 1980). By 1997/8 rates of ownership for all cohorts are close to 100 percent. Clearly, the propensity to purchase telephones does not decrease with age in any of these cohorts.

Although, as Figure 6.4 shows, rates of TV ownership are much higher than those for phones for all cohorts at the beginning of the period for which there is data the trend toward increasing ownership across time is the same. Again, it is the oldest and youngest cohorts that have the lowest rates in 1968 and in 1973, the first time point for which there is data available, it is the second baby boom that has the lowest rates. However, by 1988 rates of TV ownership are at or close to 100 percent for all cohorts. Again, there is no evidence that rates of ownership decline as each cohort ages.

Figure 6.3
Phone Ownership by Pseudo-Cohort 1968-2004/5

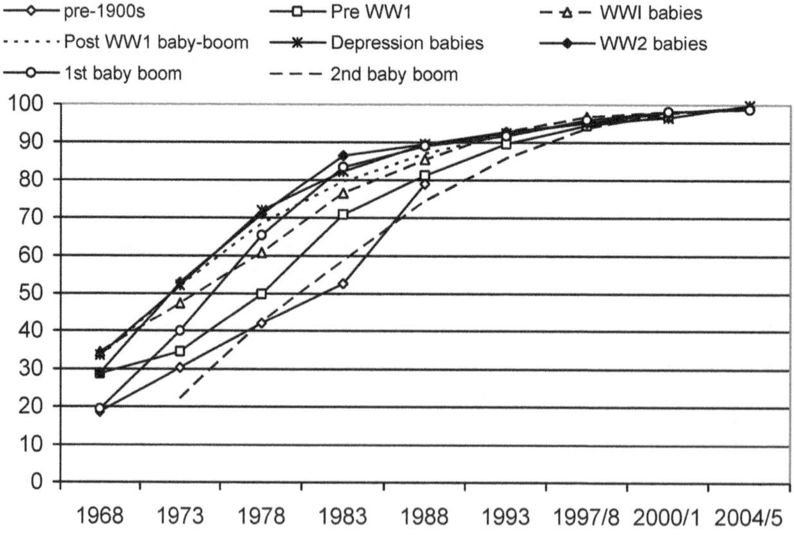

Figure 6.4
TV Ownership by Pseudo-Cohort 1968-2004/5

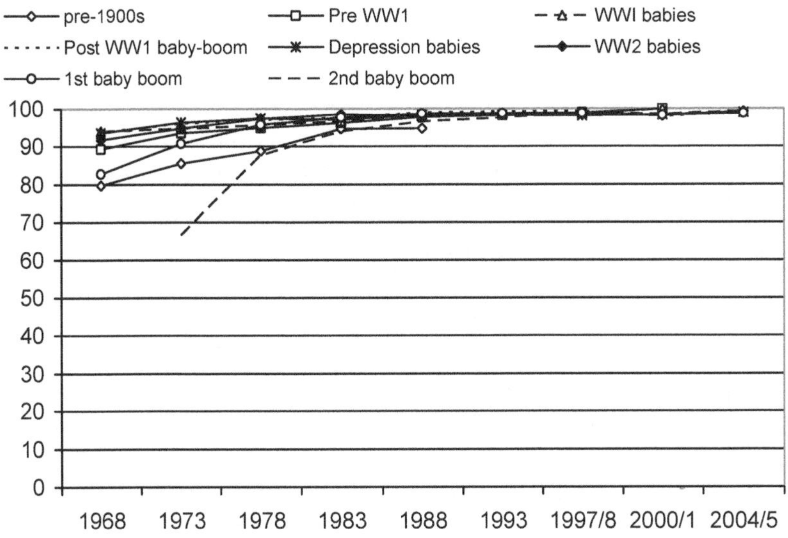

—◇— pre-1900s   —□— Pre WW1   – ▲ – WWI babies
· · · · · · Post WW1 baby-boom   —✱— Depression babies   —◆— WW2 babies
—○— 1st baby boom   – – – 2nd baby boom

Trends in car ownership, as displayed in Figure 6.5, show a markedly different pattern than either phone or TV ownership. Here it is clear that older cohorts tend to have lower rates of car ownership at each point in time. For example, in 1968 only around 20 percent of households headed by someone born between 1880 and 1899 had a car, compared to over 70 percent of those who were born during World War Two. Younger cohorts also show greater increases in ownership than older cohorts, although this might in part be explained by already high levels of ownership in these older cohorts. In 1978, around 40 percent of households headed by someone born between 1955 and 1965 had a car, compared to about 70 percent of those born during the Depression. However, by 1988 the rate among the former had shot up to over 70 percent, whilst that for the latter had increased to just under 80 percent. However, as cohorts age there is a clear downward trend in ownership following this increase for all but the youngest two cohorts and the pre-WWI birth cohort. For example, rates of ownership amongst the World War One birth cohort fall dramatically from 60 percent in 1988 to around 35 percent in 1993 and, although the

Figure 6.5
Car-Ownership by Pseudo-Cohort 1973-2004/5

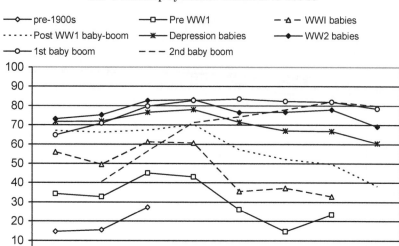

severity of the decline is weaker, for younger cohorts this pattern is still evident.

Turning to ownership of novel goods one sees that all cohorts report rising rates of VCR ownership from 1988, the earliest time point for which there is data on this, to 2000/1 (Figure 6.6). However, there are clear inter-cohort differences in rates of ownership with younger cohorts tending to have higher rates at all points in time. The exception to this is in 1988 when the rate of ownership amongst the "second baby boomers" is just over 60 percent, which is lower than that for both the WWII birth cohort and the first baby boomers. However, as this cohort ages the rates of ownership rise steadily and rapidly overtaking the WWII babies by 1993 and the first baby boomers by 2000/1. By 2000/1 there is little difference among the youngest four cohorts with rates of ownership converging around 90 percent. Lastly, although there appears to be a flattening out of ownership rates, from 1997/8 onwards there is, unlike the trends for car ownership, little evidence that rates decline as these cohorts age. The exception to this is the post-WWI baby boom cohort where rates decline slightly from 2000/1 to 2004/5.

Figure 6.6
VCR Ownership by Pseudo-Cohort 1993-2004/5

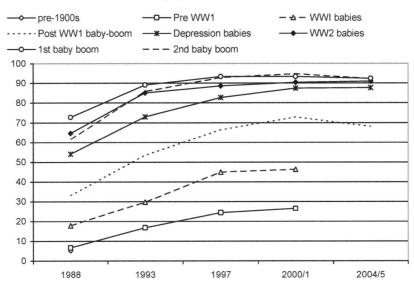

For microwave ownership (shown in Figure 6.7) it is clear that at almost all points in time, those in the older cohorts have the lowest rates of ownership. The exception is for those in the second baby boom in 1993, which has slightly lower rates than either the WWII birth cohort or the first baby boom. However, by 2000/1 both post-WWII baby boom cohorts have the same rate of ownership, around 90 percent, which is over twice as large as that for those born before WWI. Yet despite these cohort differences, there is no evidence of a decline in the rates of ownership within cohorts over the period.

As with microwave ownership there is a clear pattern of inter-cohort differences in dishwasher ownership (Figure 6.8) with younger cohorts, in general, exhibiting higher rates of ownership at all points in time. However, unlike microwave ownership, although there is evidence of a slight increase in rates of dishwasher owner-ship amongst the youngest three cohorts; the trends are somewhat flatter for all other cohorts. For example, in 1993 figures for the rates of dishwasher ownership for those in the pre-WWI and WWI birth cohorts were 3 and 4 percent respectively. By 2000/1 these

Figure 6.7
Microwave Ownership by Pseudo-Cohort 1993-2004/5

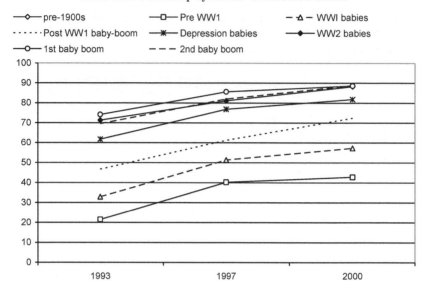

Figure 6.8
Dishwasher Ownership by Pseudo-Cohort 1993-2004/5

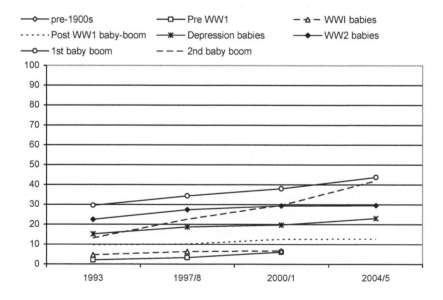

Figure 6.9
PC Ownership by Pseudo-Cohort 1993-2004/5

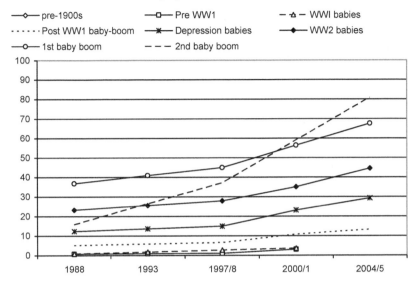

figures had only risen to 7 percent for both cohorts. By contrast, the rates of ownership amongst those born during the second baby boom rose from around 14 percent in 1993 to over 40 percent in 2004/5.

The pattern for rates of PC ownership (Figure 6.9) clearly show widening differences between the birth cohorts. Rates of ownership are low to begin with and remain low for the oldest two cohorts. Subsequent cohorts show progressively steeper increases in ownership over the twenty-seven-year period from 1988 to 2004/5. For all these cohorts, 1997/8 appears to be a real turning point as rates increase more rapidly following this. For example, for the WWII babies the rate of ownership increases from 23 percent in 1988 to 27 percent in 1997/8, but then rises quickly to 35 percent in 2000/1 and then on to 45 percent in 2004/5. Yet the most dramatic rise is amongst the second baby boom where rates increase rapidly and exceed those of the first baby boom by 2000/1. Furthermore, there is no evidence of any age related decline in rates of ownership for any cohort.

Finally, considering expenditure, there has been a general down-ward trend in the proportion of expenditure devoted to food for all cohorts (Figure 6.10). However, inter-cohort differences are evident at each time point with younger cohorts spending a lower proportion of their overall expenditure on food.

The trends for expenditure on fuel are somewhat different (Figure 6.11). Amongst the younger cohorts, from the Depression babies onwards, expenditure remains quite stable across the period at between 5 and 7 percent of total expenditure. Trends amongst the older cohorts show a slight but steady increase as they age. However, this goes into reverse after 1993 and by 1997/8 the proportion of expenditure is close to what it was in 1968 at just under 10 percent.

All cohorts show a steady decline in the proportion of expendi-ture devoted to clothing from 1968 to 2004/5 (Figure 6.12). Small inter-cohort differences are evident but the direction is different from either food or fuel. Younger cohorts tend to spend slightly higher proportions of their total expenditure on clothing. For ex-

Figure 6.10
**Expenditure on Food as a Proportion of Total Expenditure by Pseudo-Cohort
1968-2004/5**

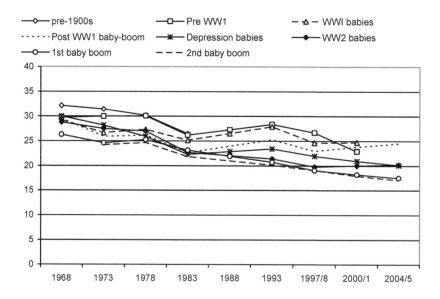

Figure 6.11
Expenditure on Fuel as a Proportion of Total Expenditure by Pseudo-Cohort
1968-2004/5

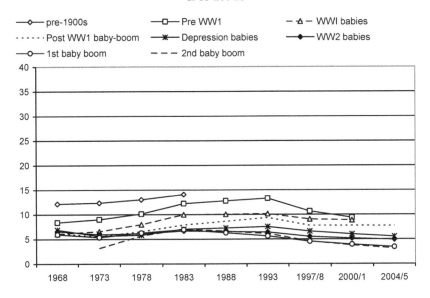

Figure 6.12
Expenditure on Clothing as a Proportion of Total Expenditure by Pseudo-Cohort
1968-2004/5

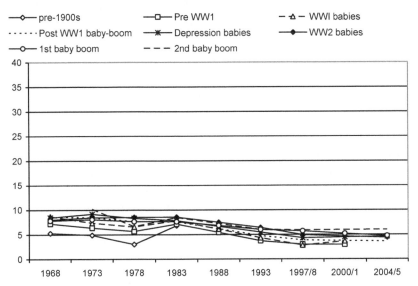

ample, in 2004/5 the second baby boom cohort spent on average just over 6 percent of their total spending on clothes compared to 4.6 percent for the Depression babies.

Figures 6.13 and 6.14 show that spending on alcohol and tobacco both follow a similar path for all cohorts. Although spending remains low across the period, at or around 5 percent, there is a general rise from 1978 to 1983. However, following this rates fall back to or lower than the pre-1978 values. The exception to this are the second baby boomers who begin (in 1973) with relatively high levels of expenditure. This could in part be explained by the fact that they are only, on average, eighteen years old at this time. By the time they reach their early twenties, their spending on alcohol has fallen in line with that for the other cohorts and remains so thereafter.

Trends in expenditure on household goods (Figure 6.15) show a very different pattern. Inter-cohort differences, with younger cohorts spending proportionately more than older cohorts, are clear between 1968 and 1983. However, by 1993 the rates for cohorts have converged. This is due to the increased proportion of expenditure spent by the older cohorts rather than falling expenditure amongst younger cohorts. However, by 2000/1 the differences have reappeared although the age related differences are somewhat reversed with the Depression babies now spending the highest proportion and the second baby boomers spending the lowest.

The data on expenditure on travel and transport shows clear inter-cohort differences. In general, younger cohorts spend a greater proportion of their overall expenditure on travel and transport. This is most evident in 2004/5 when both baby boomers spent around 16 percent compared to the post WWI baby boomers who spent just 9.5 percent. There is also evidence of an age related decline in spending amongst all but the youngest two cohorts. This, however, might be partially explained by the fact that many people become eligible for concessionary or free travel once they reach sixty.

Conclusion

Our findings show that retirees are increasingly engaged in consumption through the purchase of household goods. These results

Figure 6.13
Expenditure on Alcohol as a Proportion of Total Expenditure by Pseudo-Cohort 1968-2004/5

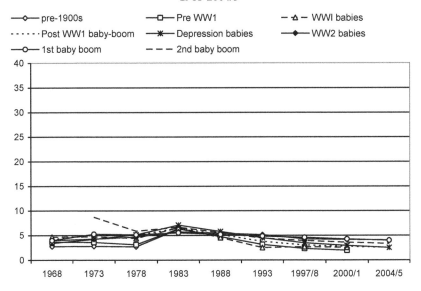

Figure 6.14
Expenditure on Tobacco as a Proportion of Total Expenditure by Pseudo-Cohort 1968-2004/5

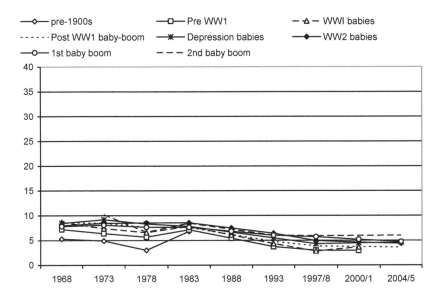

Figure 6.15
Expenditure on Household Goods as a Proportion of Total Expenditure by
Pseudo-Cohort 1968-2004/5

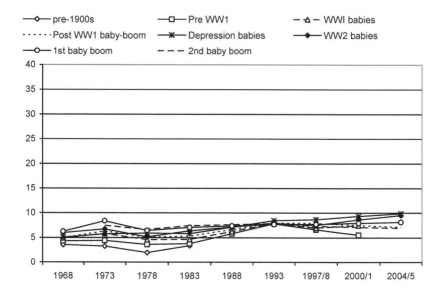

update and confirm those found elsewhere in the UK (Blow, Leicester, and Oldfield, 2004). Although engagement with consumerism is likely to be uneven and differentiated by other socio-economic factors within this group, retirees can no longer be seen as a distinct group excluded from consumer society. Whilst these data do much to support the argument that later life is becoming increasingly defined by leisure and consumption (Gilleard and Higgs, 2000; 2005) they do little to address the main cause of these changes.

Although any attempt to address these issues empirically will suffer from an under-determinacy of data, the analyses of the patterns of ownership and expenditure do reveal some important clues. Firstly, the lack of any age-associated decline in ownership of most goods suggests that this has become a generalized phenomenon and not simply restricted to the baby boomers. This is further supported by the general trend towards convergence in rates of ownership of items like telephones and TVs. In fact, a large part of this convergence in established goods is due to the baby boomers catching up with the already relatively high rates of ownership in other cohorts.

Car ownership tells a somewhat different story as there is some evidence of age-associated decline, especially amongst the older cohorts. However, this may in part be explained by failing health and the fact that women in these cohorts, who are more likely to survive into older ages, are much less likely to have learned to drive than those in younger cohorts.

Whilst there is little evidence of age associated decline in the ownership of novel goods, there does appear to be some evidence to suggest that increased levels of ownership of these goods are being driven by the baby boomers. This trend is especially evident in PC ownership, where the gap between the two boomer cohorts and the others appears to be widening rather than narrowing.

Inter-cohort differences in expenditure are evident with older cohorts seeming to spend slightly higher proportions on basic categories, such as food and fuel, than those in the younger cohorts. In turn, there is some evidence to support the argument that baby boomers spend more on luxury or leisure goods, such as household goods. This would support the evidence on the higher rates of ownership of personal and entertainment items like VCRs and PCs amongst these cohorts. However, overall it is very difficult to identify any particular cohort as having distinctive expenditure patterns.

Thus, the evidence presented here seems contradictory. There appears to be support for the generational hypothesis when one looks at ownership of established goods and, to some extent, expenditure. However, the data on novel goods appears to support the cohort hypothesis. It seems that when a product begins to reach a certain critical mass in the market, cohort differences are no longer evident, but, thus far, the uptake of new products amongst older people is being pioneered by the younger cohorts. However, as these new products become more widely owned perhaps we will see the collapse of these cohort boundaries as well.

References

Abrams, P. (1970). "Rites de passage: The conflict of generations in industrial society." *Journal of Contemporary History*, 5: 175-190.

Allen, S., Beales, S., Busolo, D., Clark, F., Eldridge, C., Gonzalez, O., Gorman, M., Hall, C., Heslop, A., Hinchliff, P., Humphreys, A., James, J., López-Clavero, C., McGowan,

L., Pannirselvam, J., and Peachey, K. (2002). "The state of the world's older people 2002." London: Help Age International.

Amin, A. (1997). "Post-Fordism: A reader." Oxford: Blackwell.

Atkinson, A. B. (2000). "Distribution of income and wealth," in A. H. Halsey, and J. Webb, *Twentieth-Century British Social Trends*. Basingstoke: Macmillan Press Ltd.

Bass, S. and Caro, J. (2001). "Productive aging: A conceptual framework," in Morrow-Howell, N., Hinterlong, J., and Sherraden, M. (Eds), "Productive aging. Concepts and Challenges." Baltimore: John Hopkins University Press.

Bauman, Z. (1995). *Life in Fragments*. Oxford: Blackwell.

Beck, U. Bonss, W., and Lau, C. (2003). "The Theory of Reflexive Modernization, Problematic, Hypotheses and Research Programme." *Theory, Culture and Society*, 20, no. 2: 1-33.

Becker, H. (1991). "A pattern of generations and its consequences," in H. A. Becker (Ed), *Dynamics of Cohort and Generations* (pp. 210-214). Amsterdam: Thesis Publishers.

Biggs, S., Phillipson, C., Leach, R., and Money, A. (2006). "Baby Boomers and Adult Ageing in Public Policy: The Changing Relationship between Production and Consumption." Working paper ESRC/AHRC Cultures of Consumption.

Blow, L. Leicester, A., and Oldfield, Z. (2004). *Consumption Trends in the UK, 1975-99.* London: Institute of Fiscal Studies.

Bone, M. (1995). *Trends in Dependency among Older People in England.* London: OPCS.

Bourdieu, P. (1977). *Outline of a Theory of Practice.* Cambridge: Cambridge University Press.

Bury, M. (1995). "Ageing, gender, and sociological theory," in S. Arber and J. Ginn (Eds.), *Connecting gender and ageing* (pp. 15-30). Philadelphia: Open University Press.

Casey, B. and Yamada, A. (2002). "Getting older, getting poorer? A study of the earnings, pensions, assets and living arrangements of older people in nine countries." OECD occasional paper, 60, OECD.

Castells, M. (1996). *The Rise of the Network Society.* Oxford: Blackwell.

Crimmins EM. (2004). "Trends in the health of the elderly." *Annual Review of Public Health*, 25: 79-98.

Cutler, N. (1977). "Political socialization research as generational analysis: The cohort approach versus the lineage approach," in Renshon S.A. (Ed), *Handbook of Political Socialization*. New York: Free Press.

Fairchilds, C. (1998). "Consumption in early modern Europe." *Comparative Studies in Society and History*, 35: 850-858.

Foner N. (1984). "Age and social change," in Kertzer DI and Keith J (Ed), *Age and Anthropological Theory* (pp. 195-216). London: Cornell University Press.

Freedman, V.A., Crimmins, E., Schoeni, R.F., Spillman, B.C., Aykan, H., Kramarow, E., Land, K., Lubitz, J., Manton, K., Martin, L.G., Shinberg, D., and Waidmann, T. (2004). "Resolving inconsistencies in trends in old-age disability. Report from a technical working group." *Demography*, 41: 417-44.

Freedman, V.A., Martin, L.G., and Schoeni, R.F. (2002). "Recent trends in disability and functioning among older adults in the United States. A systematic review." *JAMA*: 3137-46.

Fries, J.F., Green, L.W., Levine, S. (1989). "Health promotion and the compression of morbidity." *Lancet*. 481-3.

Fries, J.F. (1980). "Aging, natural death and the compression of morbidity." *New England Journal of Medicine*, 303: 130-5.

Fries, J.F. (2003). "Measuring and monitoring success in compressing morbidity." *Annals of Internal Medicine*, 139: 455-9.

Gee, E. and Gutman, G. (2000). Population and politics: Vodoo demography, population aging and social policy, in E. Gee and G. Gutman (Eds), *The overselling of population aging: Apocalyptic demography, intergenerational challenges, and social policy.* Oxford: Oxford University Press.

Giddens, A. (1991). *Modernity and Self-identity: Self and Society in the Late Modern Age.* London: Polity Press.

Gilleard, C. and Higgs, P. (2000). *Cultures of Ageing: Self, Citizen and the Body.* Harlow: Prentice Hall.

Gilleard, C. and Higgs, P. (2005). *Contexts of Ageing: Self, Citizen and the Body.* Cambridge: Polity Press.

Gordon, C.C. and Longino, C.F., Jr. (2000). "Age structure and social structure." *Contemporary Sociology*, 29: 699-703.

Guillemard, A.M. and Rein, M. (1993). "Comparative patterns of retirement—recent trends in developed societies." *Annual Review of Sociology,* 19: 469-503.

Gunter, B. (1998). *Understanding the Older Consumer: The Grey Market.* Routledge, London.

Hardy, M.A. and Waite, L. (1997). "Doing time: reconciling biography with history in the study of social change," in Hardy M.A. (Ed), *Studying Aging and Social Change* (pp. 1-21). London: Sage Publications.

Huber, J. and Skidmore, P. (2003). *The New Old. Why Baby Boomers Won't Be Pensioned Off.* London: Demos.

Irwin, S. (1999). "Later Life, Inequality and Sociological Theory." *Ageing and Society*, 19, no 6: 691-715.

Jackson, W.A. (2006). "Post Fordism and Population Ageing." *International Review of Applied Economics*, 20: 449-67

Kertzer, D. (1983). "Generation as a sociological problem." *Annual Review of Sociology*, 9: 125-49.

Kohli, M. and Rein, M. (1991). "The changing balance of work and retirement." In: Kohli, M., Rein, M., Guillemard, A.M., and Van Gunsteren, H. (Eds), *Time for Retirement. Comparative Studies of Early Exit from the Labor Force* (pp. 1-35). Cambridge: Cambridge University Press.

Kohli, M. and Meyer, J.W. (1986). "Social-structure and social construction of life stages." *Human Development, 29:* 145-149

Kotlikoff, L.J. and Burns, S. (2005). *The coming generational storm. What you need to know about America's economic future.* London: MIT.

Laczko, F. and Philipson, C. (1991). *Changing Work and Retirement.* Milton Keynes: Open University Press.

Lash, S. and Urry, J. (1987). *The End of Organized Capitalism.* London: Polity Press.

Laslett, P. (1996). *A Fresh Map of Life,* (2nd edition). London: MacMillan Press.

Lloyd-Sherlock, P. (2002). "Social policy and population ageing: challenges for North and South." *International Journal of Epidemiology*, 31: 754-7.

Mannheim, K. (1952). "The Problem of Generation," in Kecskemeti, P. (ed.), *Essays on the Sociology of Knowledge.* London: Routledge.

Manton, K.G. and Land, K.C. (2000). "Active life expectancy estimates for the U.S. elderly population: A mulitdimensional continuous-mixture model of functional change applied to competed cohorts." *Demography*, 37: 253-65.

Manton, K. G. and J. W. Vaupel. (1995). "Survival after the age of 80 in the United States, Sweden, France, England, and Japan." *New England Journal of Medicine* 333: 1232-1235

Minicuci, N. and Noale, M. for the ILSA group. (2005). "Influence of level of education on disability free life expectancy by sex: the ILSA study." *Experimental Gerontology*, 40: 997-1003.

OECD. (2007). Pensions at a glance. Paris: OECD.

Oldenziel, R. de la Bruhèze, A.A.A., and de Wit, O. (2005). "Europe's Mediation Junction: Technology and Consumer Society in the 20th Century." *History and Technology*, 21: 107-139.

Palmore, E. (1978). "When can age period and cohort be separated?" *Social Forces*, 51: 282-295.

Pierson, P. (2001). "Post industrial pressures on the mature welfare states," in: Pierson, P. (ed), *The New Politics of the Welfare State* (pp. 80-104). Oxford University Press, New York.

Polivka, L. (2001). "Globalization, population aging and ethics." *Journal of Aging and Identity*, 6: 147-63.

Reyes-Ortiz, C.A., Ostir, G.V., Pelaez, M., and Ottenbacher, K.J. (2006). "Cross-national comparison of disability in Latin American and Caribbean persons aged 75 and older." *Archives of Gerontology and Geriatrics*, 42: 21-33.

Rowe, J.W. and Kahn, R.L. (1998). *Successful aging.* New York: Dell Publishing.

Ryder, N.B. (1985). "The cohort as a concept in the study of social change," in Mason W.M. and Fienberg, S.E. (Eds), *Cohort Analysis in Social Research. Beyond the Identification Problem* (pp. 9-44). New York: Springer-Verlag.

Ryder, N.B. (1997 [1965]). "The cohort as a concept in the study of social change," in M.A. Hardy (Ed), *Studying Aging and Social Change* (pp. 66-92). London: Sage Publications.

Sassatelli, R. (2007). *Consumer Culture; History, Theory and Politics.* London: Sage.

Scheidt, R.J., Humphreys, D.R., and Yorgason, J.B. (1999). "Successful aging: What's not to like?" *The Journal of Applied Gerontology*, 18: 277-82.

Smith, J.W. and Clurman, A. (1997). *Rocking the Ages: The Yankelovich Report on Generational Marketing.* New York: HarperCollins.

Stearns, P.N. (1997). "Stages of consumerism: Recent work on the issues of periodization." *Journal of Modern History*, 69: 102-117

Strausser, S. McGovern, C., and Judt, M. (Eds) (1998). *Getting and Spending, Europe and American Consumer Societies in the 20th Century.* Cambridge: Cambridge University Press.

Taylor-Gooby, P.F. (2002). "The silver age of the welfare state: Perspectives on resilience." *Journal of Social Policy*, 31: 597-622.

Trentmann, F. (2004). "Beyond Consumerism: New Historical Perspectives on Consumption." *Journal of Contemporary History*, 39: 373-401.

Turner, B.S. (1989). "Ageing, politics and sociological theory." *British Journal of Sociology*, 40: 588-606.

UN. (2002). *World Aging 1959-2050.* Geneva, United Nations Population Division.

Vaupel, J.W. (1997). "The remarkable improvements in survival at older ages." *Philosophical Transactions: Biological Sciences*, 352: 1799-1804.

Vincent, J. (2005). "Understanding generations: political economy and culture in an ageing society." *British Journal of Sociology*, vol 46: 579-99.

Warnes (2006). "The future life course, migration and old age," in Vincent, J., Phillipson, C., and Downs, M. (Eds), *The Futures of Old Age.* London: Sage.

White, H. (1992). "Succession and generations: looking back on chains of opportunity," in H. A. Becker (Ed), *Dynamics of Cohort and Generations Research.* Amsterdam: Thesis Publishers.

Whitlier, N. (1997). "Political generations, micro-cohorts and the transformation of social movements." *American Sociological Review*, 62: 760-78.

Wittenberg, R., Pickard, L., Comas-Herrera, Davies, B., and Darton, R. (2001). "Demand for long-term care for older people in England to 2031." *Health Statistics Quarterly*, 12: 5-17.

Wilson G. (2002). "Globalization and older people: effects of markets and migration."
   Ageing and Society, 22; 647-63
Yeandle, S. (2003). "The international context," in Alcock, P., Beatty, C., Fothergill, S.,
   Macmillan, R., Yeandle, S., (Eds), *Work to Welfare. How Men became Detached from
   the Labour Market*. Cambridge: Cambridge University Press.

Part III

International Comparisons of Changes in Consumption Patterns across Generations

7

Housing Crisis, Generational Inequalities, and Welfare States

Fanny Bugeja

Comparative Research between France and the United Kingdom

In the past twenty-five years, in France, the share of housing expenses incurred by households in their total budget has increased considerably. It became the first budgetary margin, far beyond food. At the beginning of the eighties, these two expenses respectively represented 14 percent and 15 percent of households' budget. In 2004, these proportions were 21 percent and 12 percent (Plateau, 2006) whereas housing can be considered as a "forced cost" (Fabre, 2007). In addition to this quantitative transformation, there is also a more qualitative transformation in terms of lifestyle. As a matter of fact, in 1980 as during the beginning of century (Halbwachs, 1912), the budgetary margin of housing (energy excluded) was independent from households' budgets. But in 2000, housing, common law, and basic good became an inferior good since the share of housing expenditure in household budgets increases when income decreases. This result suggests that the more underprivileged categories of population have recently been constrained by the pressure of housing in their budgets.

French society has often been characterized by generational inequalities (Chauvel, 1998) whereas this is absolutely not the case for British society. Actually, in France, new generations are underprivileged in many ways (job market, unemployment, level of wages) whereas the baby boom generation—born between

1940 and 1950, the golden decade—has benefited for life from the progress and the growth of "*Les Trente Glorieuses*" ("The Glorious Thirty," 1945-1975). This observation leads us to study housing from the point of view of generational inequalities.

The aim of this research is to test the hypothesis according to which French society, as a corporatist model, is more inclined to produce intergenerational inequalities in terms of housing pressure whereas British society, as a liberal model, produces strong intra-generational inequalities in terms of housing constraint.

To answer these questions, the present chapter is organized as follows. The first part describes the methodology and the indicator used. The second part analyses the link between welfare states and generational inequalities in terms of housing. The third explains the main differences in the housing systems in both countries. The fourth studies the link between housing tenure forms and genera-tional inequalities. And, the last one deals with the articulation between housing constraint and generational inequalities.

Methodology

The study is based on a statistical analysis of the Family Expen-ditures Survey for the United Kingdom and "*l'enquête Budget de Famille*" for France. The idea of this study is to analyze the evolu-tion of the housing constraint over twenty years. So, I have at my disposal surveys of 1985 and 2005 for each country.

The main indicator I use to analyze the pressure of housing expenditure is the budgetary margin of housing by the number of rooms (bathroom, small kitchen, and WC excluded) where the budgetary margin of housing is the share of housing expenses (rent, mortgage, maintenance costs, tax, and insurance linked to housing) and fuel, light, and power expenses in total expenditure per capita in the household in total expenditure. This housing expenditure concerns main and second dwellings. This consideration does not result from a choice, it is linked to the fact that the distinction is not systematically made in the data I have at my disposal. The choice of this indicator results from the fact that it allows us to "relativ-ize" the constraint imposed on the categories of population by the increase in the price of dwelling since it controls two aspects of housing condition: the number of persons and the number of rooms in the accommodation. Actually, the major research that studies the housing constraint takes into account the share of housing expense in the total budget. If some of these indicators control the effect of the number of persons in the household by the consumption unit, it does not integrate the number of rooms in the dwelling. The following statistical analysis is on the entire sample. A distinction between types of tenure is not made and the analysis includes homeowners without a mortgage. The consideration of this category in my sample might seem paradoxical but, in studying the generational inequalities, it is important to integrate homeowners because they reflect and create inequalities in the housing market.

So, this research, using the budgetary margin of housing as part of the indicator, comes within the framework of Halbwachs who based his research on this analysis of the budgetary margin to explain lifestyles (Halbwachs, 1912).

Welfare Regimes and Generational Inequalities in Terms of Housing

This question of generational inequalities makes sense in a comparative study between France and the United Kingdom since the differences between both welfare regimes seem to have divergent effects in terms of generational inequalities.

In reference to Esping-Andersen's classification of welfare regimes (Esping-Andersen, 1999) the United Kingdom, as all the Anglo Saxon countries, can be characterized as a liberal or residual regime and France as a conservative or corporatist regime. In the United Kingdom, the economy is based on a "laissez-faire" ("let do") ideology, the welfare state as residual, social stratification reflects the competitive market, the retirement system is a funded pension scheme (*retraite par capitalisation*) and social protection is minimal. Conversely, in France, the welfare state redistributes more, the retirement system is a pay-as-you-go system based on social policy (*retraite par repartition*), and the social security net is directly linked to professional status.

The effects of these differences between the welfare regimes in terms of generational inequalities have been little studied.

Cecile Van de Velde, basing her study on André Masson's generational analysis of welfare regimes, explains that the question of generational transfers is specific to a corporatist model. Indeed, in terms of retirement, the social policy according to which the working population finances the retirement of the older involves generational solidarity and interdependency. So, on the one hand, children finance their elders through social policy and, on the other hand, parents take care of their children—depending on their financial means and their social position (Van De Velde, 2007). Consequently, the young French people, directly touched by a massive rate of unemployment (22.3 percent in 2005 for the fifteen to twenty-four-year-olds compared to 12.9 percent in the United Kingdom [INSEE]) have to make a choice between higher and further education with parental financial assistance or entering the labor market early without further qualifications and risking insecure jobs with low incomes. The consequences in terms of housing for young households might be a polarization between those who benefit from parental assistance and those who do not benefit from it. This second group is at risk of difficulties in finding lodgings (high deposit required, "caution") and then struggling to pay their rents that have never been so high. In this way, French society seems to produce generational inequalities at the expense of new generations and young people.

Conversely, in the United Kingdom, transfers between generations are supposed to be regulated by actuarial neutrality since each cohort finances its own survival on the job market (Van De Velde, 2007). Consequently, the question of generations may have less relevance in a liberal model. Moreover, the weakness of the social protection, the system of funded pensions, and the competition between workers can create a polarization between insiders and outsiders. The practices of French and British youths in terms of job position are consequently different. British youths are encouraged to enter the job market earlier or to alternate education with jobs. This model seems to be more inclined to produce intra-generational inequalities since individuals within an age group are in direct competition. In terms of housing, the very poor in the fringes of the job market risk being more sensitive to the current housing crisis.

We now turn to examine the main differences in terms of housing systems between France and the United Kingdom.

The Differences in the Housing Systems of France and the United Kingdom

There are as many differences as there are similarities, the first similarity being the tension in the real estate market (Massot, 2003). Then, the relation toward homeownership is very different, which enriches the analysis.

The main common points are that the two countries have high-density populations, the stock of dwellings is comparable, and the number of individuals by housing is identical. Another similarity is the importance of the capital city, which concentrates more people than the other urban units. Nevertheless, the contrast with the other areas is more marked in the United Kingdom than in France. Consequently, the hierarchy in real estate values is more significant. Moreover, in both countries, the private or individual house is the privileged type of residence even if the individual house rate is higher (80 percent) in the United Kingdom than in France (56 percent). This result is related to higher homeownership rates. As for the differences in the housing system, there are three main points to consider.

Acquisition System

The practices in terms of credit are totally different. In the UK, it is usual to resort to mortgages with adjustable rates. Conversely, in France, it is usually the loan on real property (*crédit immobilier*) with a fixed interest rate. Then, the renegotiation, which permits mortgage equity withdrawal (*extraction de valeur immobilère*) and other goods financing, is easier in the UK than in France. But the adjustable rate mortgage represents a higher risk and a direct connection with the real estate market. It is the reason why during the beginning of the nineties when the housing prices decreased, the number of repossessions of real estate was very high (Hamnett, 2003). The term of the loan is longer (twenty-three years in average in 2002) in the UK than in France (fifteen years in average) although the length of terms is increasing in France. All these results are linked to the amount of household debt as an average of the gross disposable income: 110 percent in the United Kingdom and 60 percent in France.

The System of Rent Allowance

In France as in the United Kingdom, there has been a shift from brick and mortar subsidies (*aide à la pierre*) to personal subsidies (*aide à la personne*). The housing benefit or "allocation logement" are a means tested social security benefit since it is intended to help people with low incomes. The French housing benefits are not specific to the rental sector as is the case in the UK. In the UK, the receipt of the allowance is connected to individual income, whereas it is linked to the household income in France. Conversely, in the UK only one person in the household can benefit from the allowance, whereas several persons can in France. A major difference is the receipt of the allowance for students. In the UK, no student (unless disabled or with children) in full time education can benefit from it. Contrary to France where the allowance is totally connected to the level of income, in the UK, among those on low incomes, the higher the income the more considerable the sum of allowance. In the same way, a person already benefiting from other allowances receives the smallest amount of housing benefit. These principles reflect the emphasis on incitements to work, which is linked to the liberal philosophy.

The Tenure Distribution

Homebuyer and homeowner rates are much higher in the UK than in France. Following from these points, we now look at the tenure distribution in more detail.

Tenure Distribution in France and in the United Kingdom

Homeownership was rarely analyzed under the point of view of inequality whereas it constitutes one of the main aspirations of French (Jacquot, 2006) and British people (Hamnett, 1999) and an element of family wealth. Moreover, property impacted on the housing conditions, on the lifestyles, and on the financial security of families. Between France and the United Kingdom, tenure distributions are very different. In 2005, in France, the home ownership rate was about 61.7 percent and 24.6 percent of them were homebuyers (households with a mortgage on real property). At the same time, in the United Kingdom, these rates were very much higher: 70.2 percent were homeowners and 40.5 percent of them were homebuyers. According to the comparative work of Blossfeld and Kurz (Blossfeld and Kurz, 2004), the British notion of "property-owning democracy" introduced by M. Thatcher is linked to the welfare regime. These authors, basing their studies on Kemeny's analyses (1982 and 1992) and on Esping-Andersen's classification (1999), draw up several conclusions about the link between dominant forms of housing tenure and welfare regimes:

- In the liberal model, private property is the favorite form of housing tenure. In fact, it represents the ideology of individual liberty, individual property right, and individual responsibility. Consequently, government intervention is considered in a positive way if it favors free-markets or provides social protection with public housing or means-tested housing benefit.
- In the social-democratic model, the homeownership sector is smaller. The collective ideology places more emphasis on housing costs being distributed to permit good housing conditions for everybody. In the ideal type, the public rental sector should not be residual, stigmatized, or only concentrated on low-income households.
- According to Kemeny, in the corporatist model, neither individualism nor collectivism is dominant. Consequently, it is not possible to make conclusions about the dominant tenure form. However, governmental commitment toward the rental sector should be higher in a corporatist model than in a liberal one.

The results about tenure described in figures 7.1 and 7.2 correspond with the previous hypothesis of Blossfeld and Kurz.

In fact, property is more developed in the UK than in France for different reasons. The first reason is directly linked to the liberal policy and particularly to the "right to buy" policies of the 1980s. This law enabled public housing tenants to buy their houses at a discount of between 30 percent and 70 percent compared to the market prices. Then, there are more different sorts of homeownership in the UK than in France: the leasehold, which constitutes a

Figure 7.1
Tenure Distribution in the UK

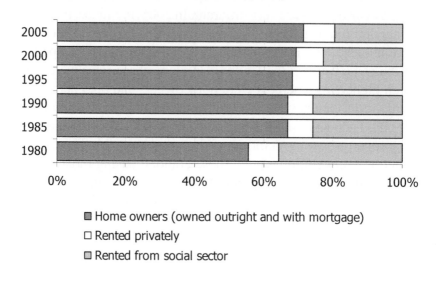

■ Home owners (owned outright and with mortgage)
□ Rented privately
▨ Rented from social sector

Figure 7.2
Tenure Distribution in France

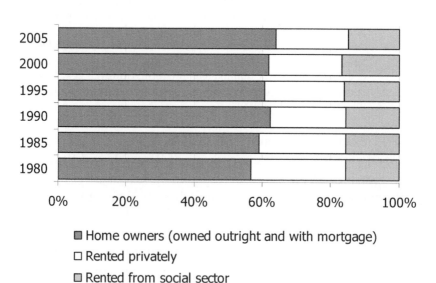

■ Home owners (owned outright and with mortgage)
□ Rented privately
▨ Rented from social sector

very widespread type of homeownership, and the shared ownership, which has no equivalent in France (Goodchild, Reid, and Blandy, 1998). Moreover, the private rental sector is residual and dualistic between timeworn and luxury supply in the UK. It represented 8.6 percent compared to 20.5 percent in France in 2005. Even if the public rental sector is quite widespread in the United Kingdom (19.2 percent compared to 14.4 percent in France, in 2005) council housing is becoming a specialized market for underprivileged groups whereas in France there is still a strong obligation towards social diversity.

If we concentrate on home ownership rates, a generational analysis also shows disparities between both countries.

According to Figure 7.3, in the UK in a static analysis, home ownership rates are not strongly linked to age group since the curve of 2005 is horizontal (excluding heads of household aged less than twenty-five years old). In a dynamic perspective, we can see homeownership has decreased for all the age groups aged less than forty-five years old between 1985 and 2005 whereas it has increased for the older age groups. In fact, this change of attitude for young households toward home ownership is directly link to the housing cycle. The housing crisis in the beginning of the nineties has deeply affected young people. Actually, the proportion of the population who identify home ownership as the preferred tenure has fallen "particularly among younger age groups, as the result of the negative equity, repossessions, falling prices and

Figure 7.3
Home Ownership Rates According to the Age of Head of Household in UK

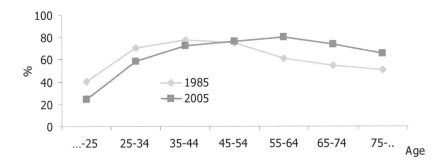

lack of confidence in the market" (Hamnett, 1999: 55; Ford and al., 2001). Even though the rates have decreased for the younger households, we will see that the percentage of homeowners was still much higher than the percentage of young French households. Consequently, relative to France, British society cannot really be characterized by intergenerational inequalities in terms of property since the recent introduction of these inequalities is linked to the housing climate.

Conversely, as Figure 7.4 shows, in France homeownership has been strongly linked to the age group for twenty years. Actually, the Pearson χ^2 shows dependence between age and tenure forms. The relation is linear; the older the head of household, the more likely they are to be a homeowner. Indeed, homeownership rates in the British households aged less than twenty-five in 2005 were four times higher than those of French households. Moreover, the old households, born during the "Glorious Thirty," have higher rates of homeownership than before. Thus, it may be argued that French society can be characterized by strong intergenerational inequalities in terms of property since this result is structural and not cyclical.

An analysis of the homeownership rates according to the quartile of total expenditure shows dependence between these two variables in both countries. The households belonging to the forth quartile (i.e., the richest) are more likely to be homeowners than the households belonging to the first quartile (i.e., the poorest). And, this

Figure 7.4
Home Ownership Rates According to the Age of Head of Household in France

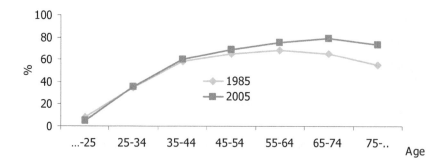

phenomenon is more pronounced in the United Kingdom than in France. So, in France, the young households aged less than forty-five, have experienced a small decrease in their homeownership rates and, on the other hand, their elders, "the gold decade," have experienced a strong increase in homeownership rates. Consequently, the *fracture générationnelle* (generational shift) identified by Louis Chauvel seems to be true also in terms of property. In fact, Louis Chauvel has already demonstrated the existence of a *fracture générationnelle* in France between the generations born before 1955 and those born after this date (Chauvel, 2006a). In other words, the parents of children who are between twenty-five and thirty-five today were more fortunate in terms of the job market and the housing market than their children who will be a "sacrificed" generation for their whole life. Is this generational phenomenon also true in terms of housing constraint?

First of all, it is important to precise that the net housing constraint indicator has increased 24 percent on average in France, whereas it has decreased almost 12 percent in the UK between 1985 and 2005. In France, these indicators were 4 percent and 5 percent, compared to 4.5 percent and 4 percent in the UK in 1985 and 2005. In terms of net budgetary margin of housing per household, the pressure of housing represents 23 percent in the UK and 24 percent in France of the household budget in 2005. So, if the housing and energy expenditure has increased in both countries, in France total expenditure has increased less quickly than the housing expenses whereas in the UK it has increased faster than housing expenditure. This disparity between both countries becomes more marked if we consider the housing constraint indicator. Consequently, the French situation of 2005 was like the British situation of 1985 and vice versa.

Housing Constraint and Generational Inequalities

Figure 7.5 shows that in France, in terms of net housing constraint, i.e., after deducting housing benefit, there is a clear age gap since the shape of the curve is convex and decreasing. Indeed, the housing constraint indicator of the younger households (i.e., the age of head of household is less than twenty-five) was 7

Figure 7.5
Net Housing Constraint Indicator According to the Age of Head of Household in
France

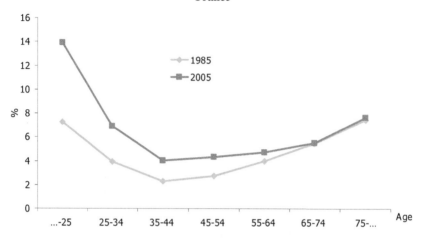

percent in 1985 and near 14 percent in 2005. Conversely, the older households' housing constraint indicator decreased near 5 percent during this period. If we compare the previous graph, which represents housing constraint indicator in net terms, with the same in gross terms, we can see that the introduction of the housing allowance does not change the distribution of the housing burden between the ages. Even if the younger householders were the main beneficiary of housing benefit, the latter was neither sufficient nor efficient. Gabrielle Fack, asking "Why do the poor households pay higher and higher rents?" (Fack, 2005), explains the automatic process by which an increase in the allowance amounts causes the same increase in homeowners' rents. The idea is that homeowners, informed about social measures, pass the allowance increase onto their next tenants' rents.

Consequently, in France, there are more and more intergenerational inequalities which are not totally reduced by the consideration of housing allowance. What is it about the British intergenerational inequalities?

Figure 7.6 shows that in the United Kingdom, we can see the pressure of housing was higher at the extreme age groups twenty years ago. Contrary to the French case, where the phenomenon is generational since it particularly concerns the younger households,

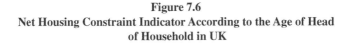

Figure 7.6
Net Housing Constraint Indicator According to the Age of Head
of Household in UK

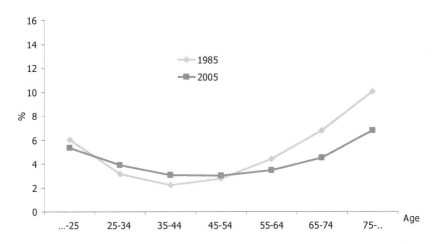

in the United Kingdom, the burden of housing is linked to age. In twenty years, the constraint for these extreme age groups has been considerably reduced, but this phenomenon of social inequality still appeared in 2005. Thus, since the younger and the older are the most constrained and are the individuals who have the weakest occupation rate too, the housing burden might be linked to the job market and the risk of unemployment. We have to note that housing allowances have a notable impact on reducing the level of constraint for these extreme age groups (the gross/net ratio in 2005 was near 1.3 for the youngest and near 1.5 for the oldest).

To sum up, French society can be characterized by intergenerational inequalities in terms of housing constraint whereas it is a picture of age or maybe labor inequalities in the UK. We can note a notable reduction of these inequalities in the UK—they are increasing in France. After studying intergenerational inequalities in terms of housing pressure, we can also examine wealth or social inequalities defined by the quartiles of total expenditure.

Figure 7.7 shows that in France, the ratio of the net housing constraint indicator between the poorest and the richest (Q1/Q4) was 4.6 in 1985 and 6.1 in 2005. The households belonging to the first and second quartiles have experienced a strong increase (about

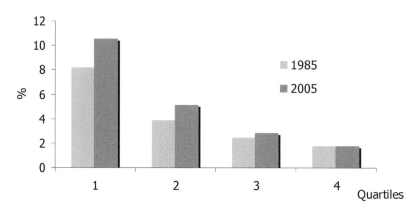

Figure 7.7
Net Housing Constraint Indicator According to the Quartile of Total Expenditure
in France

30 percent in their budgetary margins) whereas the households belonging to the fourth quartile have experienced a decrease of 2 percent in twenty years. If the housing allowances improve the situation, the presence of strong wealth inequalities in terms of housing was still clear in 2005. Currently, it seems quite obvious that the burden of housing decreases with the household's budget, but it is important to recall that it is a new phenomenon. In France in 1980, the budgetary margin of housing (energy excluded) was independent from the household's budget. Compared to generational inequalities, the level of constraint is still clearly weaker for the poorest households than for the youngest. The main phenomenon of inequalities in terms of housing constraint is strongly more generational than social.

Figure 7.8 shows that in the UK the ratio of the housing constraint indicator between the poorest and the richest (Q1/Q4) was 6.8 in 1985 and 5.7 in 2005. So, compared to the French case, the level of inequality has reduced in the UK up to 2005, whereas the poorest British households have experienced a strong fall in the constraint over twenty years. In gross terms, i.e., without deducing allowances, these ratios are very higher (8.5 in 2005). Allowances seem to have a real and significant impact on the reduction of wealth inequalities since the poor households have experienced a decrease in their housing constraint indicator of more than 18

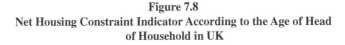

Figure 7.8
Net Housing Constraint Indicator According to the Age of Head
of Household in UK

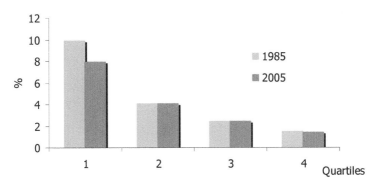

percent. Contrary to the French case where allowances mainly concern the poorest, the British system is wider and more generous than in France. This result can seem paradoxical since the means-tested and the stigmatization of the poorest by national assistance are commonly liberal and Anglo Saxon characteristics (Kurz and Blossfeld, 2004). The improvement in the situation of the poorest group has to be relativized since they are the most indebted and consequently the most vulnerable to an interest rate or increases in unemployment (Newhouse-Cohen, 2003). Moreover, I do not have at my disposal information about housing conditions. To sum up, although Figure 7.8 clearly describes a reduction of the constraint for the poorest, the wealth inequalities were still strong in 2005. Does this figure hide other sorts of inequalities? Within the poorest group, does a polarization exist which opposes workers and non-workers or "good non-workers" and "bad non-workers" (Rodriguez, 1999)? Can this phenomenon of polarization appear through an intra-generational analysis?

Figure 7.9 clearly describes two groups since at the top; we can see the poorest households belonging to the first quartile of total expenditure and at the bottom the richest (fourth quartile). Each of the poorest households in an age group had to spend a higher share of their total expenditure than the richest in order to have a dwelling when the number of persons and rooms are controlled whereas they are the first beneficiary of housing benefit. And this

Figure 7.9
Net Housing Constraint Indicator According to the Quartile of Total Expenditure in an Age Group in France

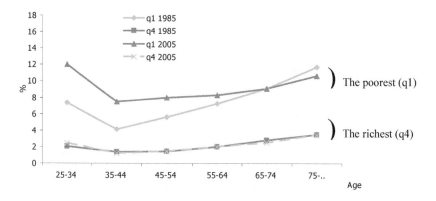

Note: The housing constraint indicator was about 8 percent in 2005 for the households belonging to the first quartile in the age group thirty-five to forty-four.

polarization became more marked in 2005 than in 1985. Moreover, we can observe the younger were the more constrained according to our conclusion in terms of intergenerational inequalities. We have seen that British society experienced a reduction in inter-generational and wealth inequalities over the twenty years and the conclusion in intra-generational terms is more nuanced. Figure 7.10 shows the polarization in age groups according to the weight of the housing constraint was less than in France in 2000. We can see that the level of constraint was maximal for the oldest households. As a matter of fact, they did not benefit from high housing benefit. If on average the housing constraint indicator has decreased, it has increased for the households belonging to the first quartile and aged less than forty-five years old. Although the polarization has reduced, it was still an important phenomenon in 2005.

Figure 7.10
**Net Housing Constraint Indicator According to the Quartile of Total Expenditure
in an Age Group in the UK**

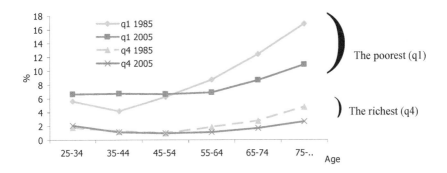

Note: The housing constraint indicator was about 5 percent in 2000 for the households belonging to the first quartile in the age group thirty-five to forty-four.

Conclusion

To conclude, our hypothesis, expressed according to Esping-Andersen's classification and to the analyses in generational terms which have been carried out, is confirmed. Our analysis has shown that in terms of net housing constraint, French society produces and has increased the production of all sorts of inequalities: inter-generational, wealth, and intra-generational since it is a corporatist model. Conversely, if the British society, as a liberal model, does not create more intergenerational inequalities and wealth inequalities in 2005 than in 1985, the production of intra-generational inequalities have increased for one category during the period and is finally very developed. Consequently, the French system of housing policy seems to be not wide and generous enough. In the UK, this system is efficient in reducing intergenerational and more particularly wealth inequalities but not intra-generational inequalities. It would be interesting to have a look at the Nordic models which are universal.

This chapter focused on the inequalities in terms of housing. It is important to note that the results may be different when homeowners are not taken into account. It would be interesting also to compare the housing constraint indicator according to the tenure group. This study is only based on the surveys of 1985 and 2005, further analysis using surveys every five years to analyze variations during the period would add to our understanding. The inheritance and family transfers aspects are not taken into account in this analysis since the surveys I have at my disposal do not permit us to study this phenomenon. It is important to clarify this lacuna since inheritance also constitutes one of the factors of housing inequality.

To conclude, we have seen that the French situation in 2005 is close to the British situation in 1985. This observation leads us to think that nothing is pre-determined and that housing constraints and inequalities could change again.

References

Chauvel, L. (1998). *Le destin des générations, Structure sociale et cohortes en France en XXe siècle.* Paris: PUF.

Chauvel, L. (2006). *Les classes moyennes à la dérive.* Paris: Seuil.

Chauvel, L. (2006a). "Social Generations, Life Chances and Welfare Regime Sustainability," in Pepper D. Culpepper, Peter A. Hall, and Bruno Palier (dir), *Changing France, The Politics that Markets Make* (pp. 150-175). Houndmills, Basingstoke, Hampshire: Palgrave Macmillan.

Elias, P. and Hogarth, T. (1994). "Joseph Rowntree Foundation, Unemployment and housing tenure," *Housing Research.* 134.

Esping-Andersen, G. (1999). *Les trois mondes de l'Etat-Providence, Essai sur le capitalisme moderne.* Paris: PUF.

Fabre, B. (2007). "Le pouvoir d'achat: discrimantes, les dépenses incontournables?" *Les ateliers de la consommation.* BIPE.

Fack, G. (2005). "Pourquoi les ménages pauvres paient-ils des loyers de plus en plus élevés? L'incidence des aides au logement en France (1973-2002)," *Economie et Statistique* (381-382): 17-40.

Ford, J., Burrows, R., and Nettleton, S. (2001). *Home Ownership in a Risk Society, A Social Analysis of Mortgage Arrears and Possessions.* The Policy Press.

Goodchild, B., Reid, B., and S., Blandy. (1998). "Accès au logement privé pour les ménages modestes: une analyse des initiatives en Grande-Bretagne," Technical report, Plan Urbanisme Construction Architecture, Sociétés urbaines, habitat et territoires.

Halbwachs, M. (1912). *La classe ouvrière et le niveau de vie - Recherches sur la hiérarchie des besoins dans les sociétés industrielles contemporaines.* Paris: Alcan.

Hamnett, C. (1999). *Winners and Losers Home Ownership in Modern Britain.* Routledge.

Jacquot, A. (2006). "Cinquante d'évolution des conditions de logement des ménages," *Données sociales, INSEE* : 467-473.

Kemeny, J. (1992). "Swedish rent-setting policy: labour-led corporatism in a strategic policy area," *International Journal of Urban and Regional Research,* 16: 555-570.

Kemeny, J. (1981). *The Myth of Home-Ownership: Private versus Public Choices in Housing Tenure.* Routledge.

Kurz, K. and Blossfeld, H-P. (2004). *Home Ownership and Social Inequality in Comparative Perspective.* Stanford University Press.

Massot, A. (2003). "Le Logement en France et au Royaume-Uni, des Besoins Croissants dans les Grandes Villes." *Cahier de l'Institut d'Aménagement et d'Urbanisme de la région Ile de France,* (35): 22-29.

Newhouse-Cohen, C. (2003). *"Royaume-Uni: vers un atterrissage en douceur,"* Conjoncture. 14-23.

Plateau, C. (2006). *"Vingt ans de dépense de logement,"* Données sociales-la société française. 475-484.

Rodriguez, J. (1999). *"La 'révolution' thatchérienne en perspective: l'Angleterre et ses pauvres depuis 1834."* Cultures et Conflits, 35: 15-34

Van De Velde, C. (2007). *"Vers un 'conflit de générations'? Jeunes adultes, dépendance économique et solidarités familiales,"* Rapport annuel du Centre d'Analyse Stratégique 2006, La société française: entre convergences et nouveaux clivages: 104-118.

8

Generational Marketing[1]

George P. Moschis

Introduction

We have been witnessing perhaps the most important demographic shift in the history of mankind—the rapid aging of the earth's population. Today, there are approximately 600 million people over the age of sixty living on this planet. By year 2050 this figure is expected to almost quadruple to 2 billion (United Nations, 2002). The number of people in the older age brackets will grow even faster (World Bank, 1994).

Two main forces have been responsible for this global aging: sharp increases in life expectancy and high birth rates in post-WWII years. In the twentieth-century, industrialized countries gained approximately thirty years in life expectancy, which is greater than what was attained in the previous 5000 years of human history. This increase was due to better public health, immunization, nutrition, and medical advances. Also, most nations of the world, especially the industrialized countries, experienced unprecedented high birth rates after WWII. In the United States, for example, birth rates during this period nearly doubled. Ninety-two percent of GIs who came back from the war got married, and 84 percent of them had children, many children—thus, the reason for the moniker "the baby boom generation."

The higher than normal birth rates that followed the post-WWII years, especially in developed countries, have been responsible for the aging cohort of baby boomers, those born between 1946 and 1964. As this cohort ages, it will swell the ranks of older age brackets, resulting in a disproportionate distribution of the age structure. By year 2030, baby boomers will be over the age of sixty-five, and, in industrialized countries, they will comprise a rather large percentage of their population. The Organization for Economic Cooperation and Development (OECD) estimates that about 15 percent of the population of the twenty-nine leading industrial nations is now age sixty-five and over. By 2030 it will be 23 percent. Germany and Italy are expected to have the largest percentage of their population age sixty-five and over (28 percent) followed by Japan (26 percent).

While the increase in the percentage of older people over the next decades represents a global trend, developing countries are expected to experience even more dramatic changes in age composition. The older population in developing nations is expected to increase by 200 to 300 percent over the next thirty years. In China, for example, the older population (age sixty plus) will double to nearly 400 million in about twenty-seven years. For some developing countries, like Malaysia and Kenya, the rate of increase in the older population is expected to be seven to eight times higher than in industrialized countries like the United Kingdom and Sweden. In the United States, the number of people aged sixty and older is expected to double by 2030 (United Nations, 2002).

The aging population is affecting just about everyone on this planet. It is affecting governments, institutions, and individuals. The aging population is putting pressure on pension funds and healthcare systems and is having economic consequences that affect economic growth, savings, and investments. This trend is also affecting families and raises issues such as elderly care giving, family composition, living arrangements, and quality of life in old age. Finally, there are a host of corporate issues raised due to the aging population, most of which fall under "workforce" and "marketing." The latter issues relate to marketing to the "maturing marketplace" because of the shifts in the age composition of the markets and their buying power.

This chapter presents a state-of-the-art assessment of marketing to the "maturing" population in the two oldest generations of consumers: baby boomers (approximate ages forty-two to sixty) and their parents (those older than sixty years of age). These two generations comprise the largest segment of consumers that is commonly referred to as "the mature market." Specifically, the chapter traces the evolution of generational marketing, with special emphasis on the mature market; it presents corporate challenges and responses to the growing sizes of these two oldest generations; it points to differences in the consumption patterns of the two generations; and suggests guidelines for marketing to baby boomers and their parents. Finally, the chapter addresses the need for understanding consumers of different generations in different parts of the globe for effectively marketing to them and offers guidelines for future research in this area.

Evolution of Generational Marketing

The term "generational marketing" is relatively new. It refers to marketing to different cohorts of people, regardless of age or stage in life. A cohort refers to a group of people within an approximate twenty-year lifespan, who were born and/or raised during different times, thus experiencing different circumstances and events in time and stages in life that other cohorts did not experience. In tracing the development of generational marketing in industrialized countries, we can identify three distinct stages of development: the prior to 1980s stage, the 1980s stage, and the stage since early 1990s.

Prior to 1980: Total Neglect

Just thirty years ago, there was hardly any evidence to suggest corporate interest in generational marketing. Untill 1980, the focus of companies had been on younger adult consumers, usually those ages eighteen to fifty, mainly because many industrialized countries, such as US, have been predominately youth oriented. Children up to age eighteen and consumers over the age of fifteen were not considered to be significant segments and were ignored. Evidence of such neglect can be seen in a number of areas, including the published research on children and mature consumers and the scarcity of products available to the mature market. Even companies that were compiling and selling syndicated studies, like A.C. Nielsen, were not gathering information on consumers younger than eighteen or older than fifty. Nearly all research published on these extreme age segments dealt with topics of interest to public policy markers, such as television advertising effects on children; the mature consumer market was viewed as an underprivileged segment of the population, having limited economic resources and significance. As a result, most corporate efforts in addressing these markets were motivated by the desire to be "socially responsible" by attending to the needs of these vulnerable, deprived, or under-privileged segments of the population.

The 1980s: Trial-and-Error Marketing

Perceptions of the consumer markets began changing around 1980. Rena Bartos' (1980) article in the *Harvard Business Review* is the first credible publication that redefined the mature market in terms of both size and buying power. In this article, she views the fifty-plus segment of the population as a "mature" market, consisting of a large number of people with diverse lifestyles and buying power. The 1980 Census also made marketers and demographers aware of the importance of the older segment of the population, showing surprisingly large numbers and wealth for the mature market.

The 1980 US Census data received a great deal of publicity by popular media and trade publications. The media coverage also mentioned the younger segment of the population, the baby boomers that comprise 78 million or 30 percent of the US population. Marketers began taking heed to these messages and developing interest first in the mature market and later in baby boomers. While up to that point in time they used to segment the market by age and stage in lifecycle, marketers began to view the market consisting not just of different age groups but rather of people born and raised during different eras. Thus, during the 1980s, nicknames for different generations or cohorts of adult consumers were coined: mature market, baby boomers, and Generation X (those born between 1964 and 1976). But since these segments of the population, especially the mature market, had been largely ignored, there was little reliable information for effective decision making. Faced with the urgency to respond to this new opportunity, many marketing decisions made by marketers, their consultants, and advertising agencies were based on stereotypes and anecdotal evidence. Companies and advertisers who made decisions based on such stereotypes learned their lessons, and there are numerous examples of companies that erred. For instance, a Kellogg's cereal product developed for the mature market and named "40-plus" was taken off the market in just six months because it stigmatized or labeled the people who were buying it as "old." It is for this reason that the 1980s can be labeled as years of "trial-and-error marketing."

1990s to Present: Increasing Refinement of Generations, Commitment, and Caution

Since the early 1990s, we noticed two trends in generational marketing. First, there have been an increasing number of companies that recognize the importance of the marketing to different generations, rather than to segments of consumers defined in terms of their age or stage in life, and developing marketing programs to effectively reach them. This is attested to by the increasing numbers of product offerings developed to satisfy the needs of these segments. It is also evident in the increasing number of companies that have organized their departments and marketing strategies by generational segments. This trend is most evident in the insurance industry.

The need to better serve the different generations prompted additional efforts to further refine these relatively large segments of the population. Thus, for example, the mature market in the US was conceived to be comprised of three sub-segments: the GI generation (the oldest consumers, born before 1930, many of whom fought in WWII), the Great Depression generation (those born and raised during the 1930s), and the War Babies (those born from 1940 to 1945). Similarly, the baby boomer generation was further subdivided into younger baby boomers (those born from 1956 to 1964) and older baby boomer (those born from 1946 to 1956). There was even a name coined for those born between 1976 and 1996—Generation Y or "baby boomlets."

The second trend is the increasing caution among marketers in designing products and messages to reach these generations. This caution is in part due to the previous marketing errors and in part due to the increasing recognition of the diversity and complexity of these generations that are viewed as "moving targets" (for reasons explained later in this chapter). As information and knowledge about these generations becomes available, marketers increasingly prefer to rely upon such information rather than their gut feelings or anecdotal evidence.

Corporate Challenges in Marketing to the Older Generations

Organizations that market products and services to older consumers are faced with both opportunities and challenges. On the one hand, the changing composition of the marketplace creates new opportunities and puts pressure on them to respond to the increasing size and wealth of the mature consumer markets, whose needs are largely unmet because they have been ignored. One of our studies, for example, found that 78 percent of Americans age fifty-five and over are not happy with the products and services available to them. On the other hand, these organizations find it difficult to effectively respond to these new opportunities due to relatively little (and often contradictory) information available about this market. I have compiled a list of questions by companies in the US based on my experience in talking to them.

1. *Should we market to older generations?* Many companies still do not see the reason they should be concerned with the mature market. Traditionally, the US consumer market has been viewed as comprised of younger people, and it is rather difficult for some companies to consider the older population as part of their main market. They may be aware of the changing demographics, but they have been slow in responding to these changes.

2. *Should the older consumer segments be treated differently?* Even when companies decide to market to the older segments of the population, many of them do not see the need to treat these segments of the population differently. They are not convinced that mature consumers differ substantially from the younger population to justify treating them as a distinctive consumer market.

3. *Should the older consumer segments be treated as a homogeneous market?* Most companies that have decided to market to the mature segment tend to consider everyone over a certain age, such as fifty, as part of the mature market and treat them the same way. They do not see the need to consider them as a heterogeneous group of consumers who

have diverse needs and preferences for marketing offerings. However, the reality is that older people are more heterogeneous than younger consumer age groups because people become increasingly different from others with age.

4. *What are the most effective bases for segmentation?* The organizations that accept the reality of a heterogeneous older consumer market are often faced with the challenging task of deciding how to subdivide this market. They consider a wide variety of bases for breaking it down into sub-segments and quite often are not sure which basis to use for effective market segmentation.

5. *How do we market to the older generations?* Finally, whether an organization chooses to market to the entire mature consumer market or to specific sub-segments, they must address a host of marketing-related issues such as:

    • What products or product modifications should be made?
    • What advertising appeals and spokespersons should be used?
    • What types of sales promotions are effective?
    • What types of services should be offered?
    • How should products and services be distributed?

In sum, they want to know what works best for the senior customer.

Marketing to Older Generations: Some Guidelines

While the effectiveness of specific marketing strategies is likely to depend on the specific segment and product or service being marketed, I can suggest a few guidelines that should be of assistance to those marketing or contemplate marketing to the two oldest generations.

1. Understand the needs of older consumers.
2. Rely on research.
3. Apply research findings in developing marketing strategy.
4. Test before implementing strategies.
5. Seek feedback.

Understand the Needs of Older Consumers

Developing an effective marketing strategy to appeal to the mature market requires knowledge about the needs of this large and diverse segment. Specifically, marketers need to understand the need states of the older consumer, how they differ from those of younger consumers, and most importantly why needs differ among consumers in the older generations.

A review of present knowledge derived from several disciplines, including marketing, gerontology, and several areas of social science suggests that differences in needs are the result of three types of factors. First, they are due to differences in aging processes, which include biophysical, psychological, and social aging. Second, the mature shopper's needs differ due to life circumstances they have experienced. Third, needs are influenced by life-changing events. The differences in the types of needs are explained in greater detail below (Moschis and Mathur, 2007).

Aging and shopping behavior. People age differently physiologically. They experience changes in bodily systems, such as declines in vision and hearing, and the onset of chronic conditions and disease at different ages and at different rates of physiological declines. Specifically, with age, people increasingly have difficulty in reading fine print and distinguishing stimuli presented in certain colors; they become more sensitive to glare, and take more time to adjust to certain light conditions; and they experience manual dexterity, which creates difficulty in holding and manipulating objects such as in opening cans, bottles, and packages. Further, as people age they experience loss in their ability to taste chemical substances—in part due to loss in taste buds and due to other factors such as increase in use of medications and loss in ability to smell. Also, with age people experience hearing loss that affects their ability to hear sounds at different frequency levels and to distinguish among certain vowels. Such physiological changes affect the way the mature shopper responds to products and services and create different needs for marketing offerings.

People also age differently socially, as they assume roles associated with old age, like the role of a retiree and a grandparent. As they assume new roles and responsibilities, they develop new needs for products and brands suitable to their newly acquired roles. Finally, psychological aging means, among other things, increasingly thinking of oneself as an "old" person; some people of a certain age are still "young at heart," while others of the same age think of themselves as old and act their age. The way mature consumers think, feel, and act their age affects their responses to products and retail offerings in general. For examples, a person age sixty-two who does not think of himself as "senior" would be offended if a clerk offers him a senior discount and would not respond to products exclusively marketed to older consumers.

Life circumstances. Consumer needs also differ due to the life circumstances people collectively experienced. Cohort and historical factors are forces (independent of aging processes) that shape shopping habits and are likely to influence the present and future shopping behavior of those in the older aged brackets. They tend to affect the mindsets of these consumers and trigger specific needs. For example, the group of consumers between the ages of fifty and sixty grew up in times when novelty and experimentation were higher on the priority list than during any prior generation. This means that while the older baby boomer might try the new product and service, such open-mindedness also makes these consumers highly unpredictable.

Life-changing events. People also tend to experience various life-changing events at different ages. As people age differently and experience various life events, they often change their outlook on life as they reevaluate their goals, wants, and roles at both personal and consumer levels. People in their forties, fifties, and sixties in particular experience a host of life-changing events, including the onset of chronic conditions due to biological aging. As a result, many consumers in these groups are likely to change their mindsets and consumption priorities due to such life-changing events. As they go through these changes, older consumer needs for products are likely to change, and so do their perceptions of, and responses to, other marketing stimuli. Our national studies conducted at the Center for Mature Consumer Studies over the previous twenty years consistently show that these life-changing events are better predictors of the person's shopping and consumption patterns than age.

The values and lifestyles of today's older generations have been shaped by the environments and circumstances they experienced, and are affecting their present shopping habits, and they are likely to affect their future shopping habits as well. The following list of *values* is particularly relevant to the baby boomer generation (Moschis and Mathur, 2007):

1.   Instant gratification—these consumers seek immediate reward; they are not willing to sacrifice or do without the main pleasures of life.
2.   Self-indulgence—they focus on "self" and "me." They consider themselves "special" in part because they have been pampered and spoiled.
3.   Ambivalent about the future—many are in debt, not adequately prepared for retirement financially, running out of time, and realizing that they may never have everything they wanted to have.
4.   Youthfulness—many of these consumers want to maintain continuity in their lives and to "preserve" their youthful self-concepts; they are terrified of growing old, defy aging, and redefine "old age."
5.   Personal fulfillment—although many are family-oriented, most people in this group tend to define themselves in terms of their work and professional accomplishments.
6.   Nostalgic—many are nostalgic of the "good old times" and years when they had fewer responsibilities.

The following are some of the *lifestyles* of the baby boomer generation (Moschis and Mathur, 2007):

1.   Health-conscious and health-driven—this group is the most health conscious age group; they report a larger number of health problems, both physical and emotional, than any prior generation of the same age. The most common lifestyle changes people in this group are likely to make are aimed at improving their health through exercising and dieting.
2.   Pressed for time—the average person in this generation is likely to lead a hectic life, trying to handle multiple responsibilities such as work, family, and care giving to older relatives. Many still have dependent children due to late marriages.
3.   Coping with stress—this group of people is the most likely to have experienced major stressful events in the recent past, such as death of a parent, and the onset of a chronic condition; they are trying to cope with such major stressful life changes and the realities of growing old. Many of their lifestyles, consumption, and leisure activities are aimed at alleviating stress.

Aging processes, life-changing events and circumstances define consumer needs, perceptions, and values that serve as "drivers" of their buying and consumption patterns. They affect the types of benefits consumers are looking for in products, the perception of the importance of product attributes, and their responses to specific marketing stimuli and shopping habits in general.

Based on changing need states over the life course, mature consumers are likely to change the criteria they use to evaluate and choose products and vendors, as well as the benefits they are seeking from consuming a product or patronizing a store. In buying products, consumers generally either try to maximize benefits (e.g., nutritional value) derived from using products or minimize problems related to product purchase and its use (e.g., ease of opening containers). The former types of benefits are primary, while the latter are secondary in importance—e.g., consumers will not buy a product they do not need regardless of how easily it can be used.

Research on Consumption Patterns of the Older Generations

Knowledge about the different and constantly changing needs states of the two heterogeneous generations of mature consumers provides the bases for developing marketing strategies. However, it is desirable to also validate the assumption that these needs, in effect, translate into different buying and consumption patterns and to supplement knowledge based on research findings. At this juncture, it would be worthwhile to present some general findings from research that has received considerable support based on several recent studies.

We have learned that, in comparison to younger generations, people in the older generations:

- Save/invest more
- Spend more on luxury products and services
- Shop during morning hours
- Prefer "one-stop" shopping
- Consider shopping to be a social event
- Are very convenience oriented
- Patronize reputable/traditional outlets
- Seek personal attention and special services such as valet parking and gift wrapping
- Choose products based on quality and brand name
- Are less price conscious and deal prone
- Use credit as often
- Are as likely to show non-significant responses to sweepstakes and telemarketing
- Complain less when they are not satisfied with something they have bought.

General Shopping Behavior of Baby Boomers and their Parents

The two groups of mature consumers differ in many ways when it comes to looking at their buying habits, whether one looks at selection of retail outlets, choice of specific products and services, or overall satisfaction with the marketplace or products (Moschis and Mathur, 2007). In this section, the terms "seniors," "elderly," and "older" are used invariably to refer to the older generation (sixty-plus); the term "younger" refers to baby boomers.

Patronage habits. Convenience is highly valued among shoppers in both groups, and it is a major reason for patronizing specific stores, especially among the older generation. Many seniors would pay a higher price to shop at a conveniently located store rather than go out of their way to save money. The importance of convenience is also shown in shoppers' preference for one-stop shopping. Again, the older generation prefers one-stop shopping more than the younger mature consumers. There are other types of convenience valued by the older generation more than by the younger shoppers, including valet parking, easy check-out, and payment methods for purchases made.

Buying products. Many people are cautious when buying products, but people become increasingly risk-averse with age. People who are risk-averse value convenience in returning merchandise. One-way consumers demonstrate caution when shopping is by showing unwillingness to buy a product without trying it first. Free samples are usually a good way of ensuring the product will be satisfactory. People in the older generations are more hesitant than baby boomers to buy a new product unless they have had a free sample; and they become more reliant on free samples as they age.

With age, older shoppers in general spend more time examining products before buying. A major reason older shoppers spend more time examining products is because they have difficulty reading information on packages and labels. Older consumers report frequent frustration with the size of lettering. However, poor vision is not the only cause of a consumer's frustration. Another factor is the ability to understand what one reads. While reading information on packages presents a problem to many people in both generations, the availability of overwhelming amounts of information can be equally frustrating. People unable to determine which products are best for them often ask store personnel for help. Shoppers who find it too difficult to discern which product is best, based on information gathered about specific products, will often use practical "rules of thumb" to decide if a product is worth buying. And because older people report greater difficulty in judging products on their merits, they are more inclined than their younger counterparts to rely on brand name and store reputation.

How do people in the two generations respond to various promotional appeals? The older generation tends to be more responsive to promotions in general than the younger mature shoppers. While the majority of shoppers in both generations admit that a special sale or discount coupon will tempt them to buy a different brand from the one they usually buy, baby boomers are those most responsive to such offerings. Although the majority of people in both generations often watch the ads for sale announcements, those most likely to pay attention to the ads tend to be older. Similarly, older consumers are more likely than younger mature shoppers to buy products because they like their ads. As expected, a larger percentage of the older generation than those in the younger age group likes ads showing products targeting older audiences. The same people who like ads aimed at older people also think there should be less advertising showing older people in situations where they are the authority figure. One reason for this may be that ads targeting older people are often in bad taste. Older people are more sensitive to age stereotypes in advertising. Many avoid buying certain products because their ads improperly stereotype older people.

Loyal customers. Who is loyal to brands and retail establishments? Loyalty to brands is a buying habit common among the majority of shoppers. Loyalty to familiar brands increases with age. Shoppers who would rather switch brands frequently than stay loyal to one brand are more likely to be older baby boomers. We have learned from many of our studies that a person may be loyal to a brand of a particular product like cereal but show very little loyalty for brands of other types of products, such as soft drinks. Loyalty to retail establishments and products is not uniform across settings or across age groups either. The older group is more loyal to various other types of retail vendors. People most likely to switch stores frequently are more likely to be the older baby boomers than any other group.

(Dis)Satisfaction and complaining. The post-purchase mind-sets and behaviors of the two groups are also interesting. In several of our studies, we examined how people feel about retail establishments, vendors, and products they have bought. We found that people in the older generation are generally more satisfied than younger adults with a large number of retail vendors. Furthermore, in analyzing how baby boomers and their parents responded to this question, we discovered that baby boomers and seniors feel the same about the different types of establishments. We also found that baby boomers complain more than older people. When we examined the complaining behavior of those who were dissatisfied, we found that eight in ten people make it a point to let others know of products and services that displease them. Finally, we looked at shoppers' satisfaction or lack of it with products in the marketplace. We found twice as many seniors as baby boomers often find packages and containers very difficult to open.

Apply Research Findings

Knowledge about consumer needs and research findings are not useful unless they are translated into implications for affective strategy in the key decision areas of market segmentation, positioning, product/service development, promotion, distribution, and pricing. Unfortunately, the effectiveness of a specific strategy is likely to vary according to the specific generation, its sub-segment targeted, and the specific product or service under consideration. Yet, there is enough information that has been generated in previous studies to suggest the desirability of certain strategies in most situations (products and segments). The following guidelines are likely to be helpful in developing strategies in main marketing decision areas.

Market segmentation. While age appears to be the most common and easiest way of segmenting the mature market, it is probably the least effective in most cases. This is because people's behavior does not correlate well with age. Instead, we found that older people's behavior is more sensitive to their needs, perceptions, and values, which are in turn influenced by aging factors, life-changing events and circumstances they have experienced. We found that segmentation based on these aging factors, life events and circumstances is more effective then segmentation based on age. This segmentation approach takes into consideration the aging process and the person's life experiences. Simply put, older people who experience similar circumstances in late life are likely to exhibit similar patterns of consumer behavior. Their consumer behavior differs from those of the older people who experienced different sets for circumstances. This approach, which is based on what I call *gerontographics* (Moschis, 1996), has produced four older consumer segments whose size (percent of the US population) has been very consistent across studies over time: the *Healthy Hermits* (38 percent), the *Ailing Outgoers* (34 percent), the *Frail Recluses* (15 percent) and the *Healthy Indulgers* (13 percent).

Healthy Hermits are likely to have experienced life events and circumstances that have affected their self-concept and self-worth. They react by becoming psychologically withdrawn. Many resent the isolation and the fact that they are expected to behave like old people. *Ailing Outgoers*, on the other hand, maintain positive self-esteem and self-concept, despite their experiencing life events such as health problems. Unlike the *Healthy Hermits*, they accept their "old age" status and acknowledge their limitations, but are still interested in getting the most out of life. *Healthy Indulgers* have experienced the fewest life-changing events such as retirement, widowhood, and chronic conditions. They are the group that differs the least from the younger generation of baby boomers. Finally, the fourth group consists of *Frail Recluses*, who have experienced the largest number of life-changing events and circumstances that denote physiological, social, and psychological aging. The four segments respond differently to marketing stimuli, justifying the development of different marketing strategies to reach each segment.

Positioning. Positioning involves the creation of an image for a product or service in the minds of consumers. It refers to what consumers think about a product or facility's characteristics or offerings relative to other similar offerings. Positioning strategy is an important aspect of marketing decision making because it defines the specific actions that must be undertaken in the areas of promotion, product development, pricing, and distribution. By positioning a product or service as having certain characteristics, it stands a good chance of gaining advantage over competitive offerings when consumers associate it with the specific characteristic(s). Our research suggests that different positioning strategies are effective for different segments of older adults. Yet, there are certain product and vendor attributes that older consumers generally value regardless of type of offering or segment. Thus, positioning a product, service, or vendor along the following attributes is likely to be effective:

- *Convenience.* The mature consumer is very convenience oriented. Convenience means different things to different people and could include location (in relation to a person's home, work, or other retail outlets), ease of doing business by phone or mail, and ease of using products and services.
- *Functionality.* Older consumers are interested in the product's intrinsic benefits, its objective characteristics, rather than subjective benefits such as what the product stands for in the eyes of others. With age, people become more introverted and, therefore, indifferent to the social benefits of the product.
- *Quality.* Older consumers are very quality-conscious. They are willing to pay a higher price in order to get a better-quality product or service. In our research we found that price becomes an important consideration only when the quality of various product and service offerings is the same.
- *Dependability.* With age, people become risk-averse and prefer hassle-free products and services. One way to ensure that they get such offerings is to buy a familiar or reputable brand or patronize a well-established and well-known retail vendor.

- *Personalized Service.* Personal attention is important to older consumers who prefer to do business face-to-face. They value the personal relationship with the service provider, and they want to know that someone within the company cares for them.

Product Development. In developing new products or modifying existing products to better serve the mature market, companies have learned that they should not develop products or attributes of interest exclusively to the older person. Rather, an increasing number of providers develop offerings that have an *intergenerational* or *universal appeal.* This means products and attributes that can satisfy the needs of both younger and older consumers but are most beneficial to the older person, such as developing easy-to-open packages and containers. Older adults prefer *products that minimize problems*, rather than products that maximize benefits. For example, a PC that has the capacity to do wonderful things may not be desirable if after-sales service or repairing it is rather inconvenient. *Ease-of-use* should be a guiding factor in product development. Also, *functionality* should be a main theme in development products and services, since older consumers are more interested in product performance than its social appeal. For example, Sears developed functional (casual) shoes for the mature market. The firm stresses "comfort" as the primary benefit and "style" as secondary. The product was not marketed exclusively for the mature market, but "comfort" is of greater interest to older adults when buying shoes.

Promotion. We have learned much over the past twenty years about the types of messages that appeal to the mature market. First, with respect to spokespersons, we have learned that older people do not relate to older models. They relate more to those chronologically younger by ten to fifteen years. Therefore, spokespersons should be considerably younger than the average age of the target market. Furthermore, when older people develop association between the product and the older user, many older people may not buy the advertised product because by buying it they would admit to their "old-age" status, and using the product would remind them of their old age. We also have learned that the aging person wants to maintain his or her youthful self-concept, so messages that reinforce the perception of being the "same person," the notion that a person of a certain age is like a person of *any* age, can be rather effective.

Also, an effective way of reducing the perception that an advertisement targets only the mature segment is to use age-irrelevant or intergenerational appeals. For example, ads for *Ensure* show a supposedly white-haired mother and her daughter using the product. Finally, nostalgia should be considered as an appeal, since older people enjoy products and services that allow them to re-live their youth.

Some additional recommendations suggested by research are the following:

- TV ads that are informative should focus only on few, key points.
- TV ads should present information at a slow pace.
- The message should be kept short and simple.
- The background/environment should be kept simple and uncluttered.
- Print media should include newspapers.
- Radio ads should be aired during news programs in early-morning hours.

Distribution. In distributing products to older adults, an organization should attempt to use a variety of distribution methods, since the older consumer market is very diverse and prefers the various distribution methods as much as the general population (with exemption of the Internet, although the older market is the fastest growing age segment of Internet users). When using a direct marketing channel such as mail order, marketers should emphasize their company's reputation, adopt policies that reduce risk (such as free pick-up services for merchandise returns), and offer a variety of payment options.

When developing traditional retail distribution outlets, the following are recommended:

- Locate retail establishments near other establishments.
- Provide adequate parking and well-lit parking lots.
- Provide rest areas, such as small café-style areas, or benches.
- Restrooms should be easy to locate.

- Use adequate lighting.
- Mark stairs with contrasting colors for easy height-change identification.
- Use services such as valet parking, gift-wrapping, and package carry-out.
- Consider innovative ways of using coupons (e.g., coupon dispensers, scanners, magnetic cards).
- Offer programs that reward long-term patrons, since older consumers are loyal customers.

Pricing. Pricing decisions should also take into account the needs and preferences of older consumers. Research suggests four general recommendations for pricing strategy:

- Offer price reductions when products and services are similar or standardized across sellers. Generally, older consumers are not very price sensitive and less likely to sacrifice quality for lower prices, but lower prices could entice them when no significant differences in product quality or service are perceived.
- Use premium pricing for drastically different products. Older consumers would pay a higher price for products suitable to their needs.
- Price product/service offerings "a´ la carte." Although older consumers are willing to pay higher prices for certain products, they are not willing to pay for product benefits and services they do not use or need. They are less likely to pay for "bundles" of benefits, when many of the benefits do not interest them. Therefore, when pricing products and services where a buyer has options, such as automobiles and cable services, marketers should make those options available for a cost rather than marketing all of them as a "package" of offerings.
- Do not over-emphasize senior discounts. Generally, senior discounts do not affect switching behavior. Seniors who use these tools buy more of the same brand or shop on different days of the week. Do not ask people to engage in activities that remind them of their old age, label them as "old," or contribute to the definition of one's self as an old person, because the reality is that nobody wants to be old.

Test before Implementing and Seek Feedback

It is prudent to test-market a strategy prior to its implementation on a large-scale basis. This can be done in a limited number of environments, such as retail outlets and geographic regions. When the strategy involves the targeting of multiple segments of the mature market, it is necessary to develop different marketing programs for different segments. In this case, a strategy developed for a specific segment should not only be tested for its effects on that specific segment, but also for any effects on other segments of the population, both older and younger. Its effectiveness should be evaluated based on its overall impact, not just its impact on the specific segment for which the strategy was developed. When a Publix supermarket in Lake County, Florida decided to appeal to the elderly by making its store more "senior-friendly" (such as making motorized carts available), it drove away the younger patrons. The retail strategy had a positive effect on older customers, but the younger people did not like to patronize a "geriatric supermarket," in the words of a younger patron.

Feedback on the effectiveness of a marketing strategy may be sought in a number of different ways depending on the product, service, or other stimuli marketed. It may be assessed by means of changes in sales volume, store traffic, and attitudes (assessed through "before-and-after" surveys). Feedback mechanisms should be made available to the mature market on a continuous basis, such as having a suggestion box or a toll-free number for complaint handling, because of the need to monitor changes in the environment such as competitors' actions and reactions.

Cross-National and Cross-Cultural Generational Marketing

The globalization of the marketplace has been creating increasing interest in marketing to consumers of different nations and cultures. Businesses that contemplate selling products and services to consumers outside their border must understand not only generational differences but also cultural differences. Knowledge about consumers in a generation in one country might not apply to consumers of the same generation in another country; and marketing strategies that have proved effective in one country might not be as effective in another.

Available cross-cultural research offers little help to international or global consumer marketers. Most commercial and academic research points to the differences in consumption habits between or among countries, but offers few explanations for the observed differences. Furthermore, many cross-cultural differences reflect differences in the ways people in different countries respond to questions or measurement instruments rather than differences in cultural values. Given the scarcity of information in this area and the need for additional research, I offer some propositions that might be intuitively appealing but they would have to be rigorously tested and validated:

1. *Today's younger generation of consumers in different countries have more homogeneous consumption patterns than previous generations.* This proposition is based on the assumption that younger people in different parts of the globe were born and raised in more homogeneous environments (e.g., mass media, retail, educational opportunities, telecommunications, and technology), and therefore they have had more homogeneous socialization experiences than older adults who were raised in more diverse commercial environments. It also suggests that, in time, consumers will become more homogeneous globally.

2. *Regardless of country or culture, the ratio of differences in the consumption patterns within generations to between generations is higher in older than in younger generations.* This proposition derives from the fairly well-established fact that people become increasingly heterogeneous with age. The longer they live on this planet, they more likely they are to experience different events and circumstances that shape their behavior and set them apart from other people with different sets of life experiences.

3. *Consumer needs driven by biophysical aging processes are more likely to be better predictors of similarities in buying and consumption patterns of people across the globe than needs driven by psychological and social aging.* This proposition is based on the premise that biophysical aging is similar in humans—programmed aging takes place in a fairly similar fashion, regardless of one's color, country, or culture. But psychological and social aging are likely to be conditioned by cultural values. For example, older adults command more respect in Eastern than in Western cultures; and their assumed roles in different stages of life might differ, as in the case of adult children who are expected to provide for their aged parents in some cultures.

4. *The greater the socio-political stability a country has experienced during the lives of its consumers, the smaller the differences in consumption patterns between generations in that country.* Social, political, and economic changes and transitions create different environments to which consumers are exposed at difference stages in their life course. Consumer exposure to diverse environments is likely to create greater diversities in socialization experiences and needs than exposure to stable environments over one's life span. Diversity is likely to result in dissimilarities in lifestyles and behaviors across generations that experience such changes at different stages in their lives, leading to different consumption patterns.

5. *There are greater within-generation differences in consumption patterns of consumers in free, capitalistic countries than in countries that have "closed" political systems.* Differences in consumption patterns are not merely a matter of individual differences in needs but also the result of options available to consumers. Consumers in capitalistic countries such

as the US and UK are likely to have more options available to them than consumers in countries such as North Korea.

Summary

The changing demographics and the aging of the population are affecting the age composition of consumer markets. This, in turn, creates opportunities and challenges for organizations serving consumer markets. This chapter has reviewed some corporate challenges and opportunities facing organizations serving the older population due to the aging marketplace. Based on present knowledge about the mature market, a list of actionable guidelines has been suggested for strategy development to effectively reach the two oldest generations—baby boomers and their parents. The effectiveness of the recommended strategies is likely to vary across situations, sub-segments, countries, and cultures. Finally, a set of propositions has been developed to guide research that would produce information useful in developing cross-national and cross-cultural marketing strategies for different generations globally.

Note

1.   This chapter is based on information contained in *Baby Boomers and Their Parents: Surprising Findings about Their Mindsets, Lifestyles, and Well-Being,* by George P. Moschis and Anil Mathur (Ithaca, New York: Paramount Market Books, 2007).

References

Bartos, Rena. (1980). "Over 49: The invisible consumer market." *Harvard Business Review* 58, (1), (February): 140-48.

Moschis, George P. (1996). *Gerontographics.* Newport, CT: Quorum.

Moschis, George P. and Anil Mathur (2007). *Baby Boomers and their Parents: Surprising Findings about Their Lifestyles, Mindsets, and Well-Being.* Ithaca, NY: Paramount Books.

UN. (2002). *Building a Society for All Ages.* Second World Assembly on Aging. Madrid, Spain, April 8-12.

World Bank. (1994). *World Population Projections.* Washington, DC: The World Bank.

9

Comparing Welfare Regime Changes: Living Standards and the Unequal Life Chances of Different Birth Cohorts[1]

Louis Chauvel

This chapter focuses on inter- and intra-cohort inequalities of living standards in a comparative perspective, and underlines the diversity of national responses to the challenges of economic slow down, stronger economic competition and globalization and their implications on different age groups. Although the paper is based on incomes and on the size of budgets more than on life styles, the relation with consumption is more than implicit since the economic constraint is the major factor affecting consumption. Here, the aim is to connect the specificities of national Welfare regimes and the emergence in different countries of very specific patterns of cohort-based economic constraints, which are about to produce, *in fine*, specific social generations (Mannheim, 1928). I highlight the emergence of "scarring effects"; that is the irreversible consequences of (short term) social fluctuations in the context of socialization on the (long term) life chances of different birth cohorts. These scarring effects can affect specific birth cohorts in countries where the welfare regime provides the context for increasing polarization between middle-aged insiders and young outsiders and is characterized by a lack of resilience to early career difficulties faced by cohorts of young adults.

In a paper on the "generational sustainability" of welfare regimes (Chauvel, 2006) in France and in the United States, I developed a comparison of the long-term consequences of welfare state reforms (see, for example, Esping-Andersen *et al.*, 2002) on different birth cohorts. The scope was to examine the concept of "social generation" as it relates to the analysis of the distribution of well-being, and to compare American and French welfare regime dynamics. The French case is marked by strong generational imbalances: in the context of economic fluctuations from the *"Trente glorieuses"* (1945-1975) to the *"Croissance ralentie"* (1975-today),[2] I have shown the existence in France of a generational rift (*"fracture générationnelle"*) between the generations born before 1955 (the early baby boom generations and the previous ones, who benefited most from the economic acceleration of the postwar period) and those born after 1955 (who are facing an economic slowdown, high youth unemployment, and the resulting social problems). Thus, we find an *"insiderization"* of previous generations and an *"outsiderization"* of new ones. That *"fracture générationnelle"* is often denied by policymakers and in the public debate; however, the long-term implications of these generational dynamics could have major consequences for the stability of our welfare state. Furthermore, if we have noticed in France the emergence of strong inter-cohort inequalities at the expense of young adults, the American answer to the same stresses (economic slow down and increasing competition) has been different: if inter-cohort inequalities are less visible, an increase in intra-cohort inequality is obvious.

My aim here is to generalize these results and develop this framework to an international comparison based on the Esping-Andersen (1990) trilogy of welfare regimes, completed by the post-Ferrara (1996) controversy, since I include the fourth Mediterranean "familialistic" model. My argument is that in the intrinsic logics of different welfare regimes, the probable set of socioeconomic responses to contemporary common challenges or stresses (economic slow down, social distortions in the face of globalization, obsolescence of unqualified or industrially-qualified labor, etc.) could be significantly different. As a clue to these differences, we notice strong cohort specific "scarring effects" in France and in Italy, when they are unclear in Nordic countries and almost non-existent in the Anglo-Saxon or liberal welfare regimes. We propose here a welfare regime based theory of international differences in inter- and intra-cohort inequalities (Mayer, 2005), since the different regimes could operate different trade offs between intra- and inter-cohort inequalities to find an answer to similar short-term stresses. These differences could directly affect the balance between and within birth cohorts, which could be marked by significantly different forms of polarization of life chances, reflected by their capacity to be organized in sets of "social generations." Finally, these different mixes of inequalities between and within birth cohorts affect durably the shape of social structures of stratification: in the welfare regimes where the cohort of young adults face an inter-cohort decline of their position, and an increase in their intra-cohort degree of inequality, emerges a risk of long term destabilization of their capacity to create or maintain a middle class based social stratification, defined as an economically homogeneous system of social strata sharing similar intermediate standards of living.

Different Responses of Welfare Regimes to Economic Stresses

To analyze more precisely the probable responses of different welfare regimes to the challenges of postindustrial societies, consider the standard typology of Welfare regimes (Esping-Andersen, 1999); we could focus on four types of regimes, respectively corporatist (or conservative), liberal, universalist (or social democrat), and familialistic:

- Since it is based on the recognition of long term and institutionalized social rights of members of protected social groups, the probable response of the *corporatist regime* (including France) to economic slow down, international competition, and economic shortage of the Welfare regime as such (as a redistributive agency, as a ruler of the labor force, and as an employer) will be a more expensive protection of insiders (stable workforce with higher seniority and high rates of trade-union memberships) at the expense of young adults leaving education, women and immigrants, who have less opportunities to defend their interests. Youth unemployment results from the scarcity of (decent) jobs in the labor market (because of the lack of competition with insiders) and the stronger internal competition of the young for obtaining less available positions generates a decline in relative or absolute wages, and specific renegotiations and retrenchments of social rights of the new social generations. If seniors are victims of early retirement, they benefit also from better protection of incomes and opportunities to access comfortable pensions schemes and/or acceptable conditions of pre-retirement (generally better than the usual unemployment schemes of younger adults). The social generations of seniors are more equal because they are the homogeneous cohorts of the "wage earner society" (Castel, 2003) of the Golden Period of 1960s-1980s (intra-cohort inequality falls for seniors), with better pension schemes developed for all (seniors relative income increases); conversely, the new cohorts of adults face a stronger polarization between winners and losers (Brzinsky-Fay, 2007; Bell *et al.*, 2007). Another aspect we do not face here is the (declining) value of education; since a probable collective answer to the difficulties of the young is a massive increase in the (postsecondary) education of young cohorts (Van De Velde, 2008) but working in tandem with a lack of improvement in labor market entry a trend of strong educational inflation (decline in the nominal value of grades, particularly for the less selective ones) can be observed (Duru Bellat, 2006).

- The *liberal regime* (including the United States) is characterized by another probable answer to the same challenges: because of the centrality of market in this regime, the response to economic shortage is Welfare State retrenchments, limitation of redistributions to worse-off populations, stronger market competition, denunciation of former social rights considered as rent-economy devices, and distortions for market equilibrium. The logic, therefore, is strengthening competition between juniors and seniors (who have less intangible rights) in order to renegotiate seniors' better positions previously obtained in the context of affluence. The consequence is smoother inter-cohort inequality (the new cohorts benefit relative to the seniors). However, strengthening competition means stronger intra-cohort inequalities. In terms of educational value, since there is a stronger linkage (by comparison to the corporatist regime of educational expansion) between the individual cost of education and the expected returns to education, the market regulation of educational expansion promotes a more stable social and economical value of grades, with no clear decline in their nominal or relative value.

- The *universalistic regime* (including Denmark) is defined by a collective scope for long-term stability, progress, and development for all with a strong sense of collective responsibility. The quality of integration of newer cohorts is then considered as a priority, since a failure in the early socialization of young adults is clearly seen as a massive problem for future development of society. Strong rates of youth unemployment and economic devalorization of young adults could go with long-term risks of anxiety, sentiment of self-devaluation of the young, increasing suicide rates, or decline in the fertility index. More generally, a better control of social risks over the complete life course is a central dimension of the Nordic Welfare State model. In terms of education, the global context of competition and massive pressure on lower and now intermediate levels of skills, the problem of old age and the necessity to maintain elders in the workforce in better conditions, all these constraints request a better distribution of qualifications over the life course and an effort of flexicurity shared by individuals and the collectivity. The consequence is a stronger control, relatively to the two previous models, of both intra- and inter-cohort inequalities. The increase in the level of education for all could generate a slight process of over-education, defined as an excess level of education in the workforce relatively to the prestige of social positions or to the level of wages, but since it is shared by all age groups, its specific cohort dimension is not obvious.

- The *familialistic regime* (including Italy) shares many aspects of the corporatist one, but families are here a legitimate institution in the process of redistribution of resources, both culturally and for the regulatory activities of the state. More precisely, in this regime, some sectors of the economy are strongly protected (mainly the core sectors of the public economy and of large companies such as banks, insurance, etc.) and most of the labor regulations are based on seniority rights; in most middle and small size companies, the regulation is based notably on family interconnections, where both localism and long term fidelity of workers are fundamental institutions. In the context of post-affluent societies, and of scarcity of jobs, housing, and other resources, parents of young adults are supposed to offer help and protection, and most families act in conformity with these social pressures. The consequence is a trend of increasing dependence of young adults until age thirty-five (or even over) in a context of declining levels of wages and standard of living for the cohorts of new entrants into the labor market. Consequently, seniors exert a political pressure to obtain better pensions, in order to support their own children. The context of dependency generates stronger constraints for young families, increases the social pressures on women to choose between work and children, and is accompanied by a strong decline in the fertility rates, which creates a paradoxical context of "familialism without families," and becomes a major problem in the long-term sustainability of the pensions and Welfare regime (shorter and less affluent careers of juniors, generational collapse of one child families, etc.). Conversely, the decline of incomes for young families is offset by the reduction of family size. In this regime, the national homogeneity may be weaker compared to other regimes since the inter-provincial imbalances (strong unemployment rates in some localities could go with a lack of appropriate workforce in others) are structural traits of a labor market where localism and strong ties are important aspects of social regulations, implying less geographic mobility. Thus, national heterogeneity is stronger than in other regimes. Another recent dimension is a strong development of mass tertiary education, which generates a strong trend towards over-education: a multiplication of university graduates who cannot find positions in the Mediterranean labor markets where middle and small size companies seek intermediate technical and managing clerks more than specialists or experts.

While the welfare regime logics and transformations are central issues, other factors could influence these results. These include:

- economic acceleration: even in the short term, a better economic situation could diminish pressure for welfare retrenchments;
- quality of the transition from school to work: close relations between the educational system and the labor market, organized internships, strong network of alumni, etc., limit the risk of "outsiderization" of young adults;
- shape of demography: a boom in fertility rates may generate twenty or twenty-five years later a phenomenon of "overcrowding" in the labor market (Easterlin, 1961; Easterlin et al., 1993).

The combinations of these factors are much more complex than expected. Because of the diversity of potential configurations, we should expect that the welfare regime explanation outlined here is only a part of the real history of each nation. While the welfare regime offers strong constraints, historical ascribed configurations (demography, level of development, and opportunities for growth, etc.) and achievements of social policies (educational booms, structural reforms on the labor market, etc.) could also be important explanatory factors.

Definitions and Tools of Generational Research

The use of "generations" in European social science is more permissive than in the American academic context: for American sociologists, "generation" refers to the sociology of kinship and to family issues, while "cohort" (or "birth cohort") refers to people born in the same year (Ryder, 1965). Therefore, in American academic journals, the expression "social generation" is quite uncommon (except in the discussions of Karl Mannheim's theories). If some economists in the American tradition (Easterlin, 1966; Auerbach et al., 1994) write about "generations" and "generational accounting," the birth cohorts they consider are also engaged in kinship relations of generational transmissions (gifts, education, legacy, etc.). The European tradition is different; here (Mentré,

1922; Mannheim, 1929) "social generation" is defined as specific groups of cohorts exposed to a common pattern of social change and/or sharing collective identity features such as ethnicity, gender, or class.

Historically, four definitions of "generation" exist (Mentré, 1922). The first one is less important to our argument: *genealogical generations* pertain to the sociology of family and kinship. The three others relate respectively to *demographic, social,* and *historic* generations. A *demographic generation* is identical to a "birth cohort": the group of individuals born in the same year. This is the most neutral clustering criterion that assumes no common trait. Conversely, the *historical generation* is a set of cohorts defined by a common culture, shared interests, consciousness of the generation's specificity and its historical role, and occasionally conflict with other generations. A historical generation may define itself by the time of its coming of age in history: a decisive example is the so-called "*génération 1968,*" which refers to the first cohorts of the baby boom (born between 1945 and 1950). The "*génération 1914,*" the generation of young adults of the First World War, is another dramatic example. *Social generation* is then defined as a link between these two polar definitions. In the empirical social sciences, we first look at demographic generations, and then we define historical generations from the results of sociological analysis, assessment, and interpretation of the diversity or homogeneity of cohorts, as well as their objective and subjective identities and consciousness.

First, we must look at "socialization" in general, without delving into a systematic theorization. During youth, between the end of school and the stabilization of adulthood, there is a specific period of "transitional socialization," which is a pivotal point in the formation of individuals' choices for the future: in a short period, usually some months, the potentialities offered by family and education turn into concrete positions from which people will construct their life courses. That individual process has collective consequences when a cultural or historical polarization has a "socialization effect" on most individual members of the new generation (Mannheim, 1929).

For people at age twenty, collective historical experiences such as May 1968 or July 1914 could form durable opportunities or scars, since they face a major transition in their lives within a dramatic social or historical context. Children cannot completely participate yet, and older people could be less affected, since they are already influenced by other experiences accumulated in other historical contexts (Ryder, 1965). This "transitional socialization" is not necessarily sufficient to create or promote durable generational traits: they need a continuous process of collective recall to reinforce the social generation's identity that would progressively vanish otherwise (Becker, 2000).

A major problem in generational social change analysis is the intersection of three social times: age, period, and cohort. The most common time is "period" and pertains to the succession of historical epochs; the second time relates to "age" and the aging process; the third one is the *time of generations*, which consists of the continuous process of replacement of elder cohorts by new ones. These three times are organized in a two-dimensional plane (see Figure 9.1) that implies a profound indeterminacy. In any given period, different age groups coexist (defined by age thresholds, age statuses, and roles), but they also represent different generations who have been socialized in different historical contexts. When we compare different age groups at a given date (period), we cannot know *a priori* whether their differences result from age or from generation: in year 2008, on the Lexis Diagram, if the age group at age sixty (born in 1948) is at the top of income scale, we do not know whether it is an age effect (any cohort will enjoy better income at age sixty) or a cohort effect (the 1948 cohort has faced the best career opportunities of the twentieth century since its entry into the labor market). Age-period-cohort models have been developed to reveal generation effects, which can be discerned when specific traits appear in the "life line" of specific cohorts (Mason *et al.*, 1973).

It is possible to mobilize Mannheim's theory of early adulthood socialization where the newer generation, which has just experienced its transitional socialization, is generally reacting strongly to new trends. In periods of sudden social change, the newer cohorts

Figure 9.1
1-Lexis Diagram

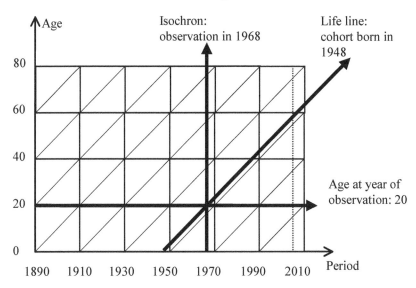

Note: The Lexis Diagram offers a synthetic view of the interactions of social times: when we cross periods, horizontally, and age, vertically, the time of cohorts appears on the diagonal (a = p − c). In year p = 2005, people at age fifty-eight are born in 1948; they were twenty in 1968. At each period, young and old age groups are also different birth cohorts for whom socialization occurred in different contexts: the seventy-five-year-old age group of 2005 (born in 1930) is also the "welfare generation" that has had abundant access to public pensions and health systems, while the same age group in period 1968 was the remains of the "sacrificed generation" born in 1893 (twenty-one years old in 1914).

are the most influenced by the discontinuities of history because they are the first to experience the new contexts of socialization that previous cohorts could not anticipate and in which they do not participate (Mead, 1970). More precisely, during an economic acceleration, the young generation of adults generally do better than older ones because they can move easily to better positions; conversely, during an economic slowdown, the newcomers are generally more fragile because they have less room in the social structure, and no past accumulation of human or social capital, nor do they possess social rights to smooth the downward shock they face. We can expect such fluctuations in the distribution of well-being by cohorts, with a succession of "sacrificed" and "elect" generations emerging over time; and if the effect of socialization is strong and durable, each generation retains the consequences of its difficult or favorable entry. These fluctuations in the distribution of well-being before any redistribution could correspond to even stronger inequalities after redistribution, since the generations marked by prosperity tend to accumulate larger contributive social rights than the generations marked by deprivation.

The Multidimensional *"fracture générationnelle"* in France

In France, the economic slowdown has provoked a dramatic multidimensional *"fracture générationnelle"* since the late 1970s (Chauvel, 2002: "Preface"; 2003). This portrait is grim, but it is founded on strong empirical bases, and alternative sets of micro-data offering convergent results. Three principal topics will be highlighted here: first, the economic marginalization of new entrants into the labor market and its direct effects on social structure; second, the long-term consequences of this deprivation in terms of socialization and life chances; and finally, the consequences for the political participation of these cohorts and their support for the contemporary welfare regime.

The Economic Decline of Youth

The first aspect of the dynamics of social generation in France is the change in the cohort distribution of economic means. A large redistribution of earnings and incomes occurred between the seventies and today. In 1977, the earnings gap between age groups thirty to thirty-five and fifty to fifty-five was 15 percent; the gap is now about 40 percent. During the *"Trente glorieuses,"* the young wage earners generally began in the labor market with the same level of income as their own parents at the end of a complete career. For the last twenty years, we have observed the stagnation of the wages of the young while wages for older people have grown by 20 percent or more. Here is a new difference between age groups, whose consequences are not completely understood by contemporary social sciences. But it is not simply a change in the relative position of age groups: members of the elder generation (now, those at age fifty-five, more or less) were relatively advantaged in their youth when compared to their seniors, and now, too, when these seniors are compared their young successors. The generational gaps result from double gains and double pains.

How could we explain this increasing gap? In fact, this is a consequence of a changing collective compromise, which occurred during the mid-1970s and early 1980s. This transition in the social value of generations arises from a relative valorization of newer generations, as a positive future we had to invest in, to a relative valorization of the protection of the adults' and seniors' stability, even at the expense of the young. The main factor in the redistribution of well-being concerned unemployment. High unemployment rates were socially acceptable for young workers, provided that adult employees with dependent children could avoid these difficulties. In 1974, the unemployment rate of those who left school twenty-four months before or less was about 4 percent; by 1985, those who left school recently had an unemployment rate of 35 percent, which remained the case through 1996; in 2002, at the end of the recent wave of economic recovery, it was close to 18 percent. The unemployment rates of recent school leavers are strongly reactive to the economic situation whereas the middle-aged and senior rates remain more stable: an economic slowdown has serious consequences for younger adults, and recovery first benefits new entrants in the labor market. Evidently, the perverse consequence of that collective compromise for the protection of adults at the expense of newcomers is the lack of socialization of the new sacrificed generations: even if they are now adults, with dependent children of their own, their unemployment rates remain much higher, and their earnings abnormally low when compared to other age groups, because of a kind of "scarring effect." At the end of the eighties, the unemployment rate of the group at age forty to forty-four was still about 4 percent and is now over 8 percent. The age compromise for the protection of adults with dependent children is unclear now. This "scarring effect" is even clearer concerning earnings: the cohorts of new entrants in the labor market in a time of downturn have to accept lower wages; conversely, for young workers, a strong economy allows them to negotiate better earnings. After this entry point, the earnings gap remains because of the lack of catch up effect on earnings (Chauvel, 2003: Chapter 3): some generations are about ten points above or below the long-term trend, because of the point at which they entered the workforce, and after age thirty, the relative benefit or handicap remains stable.

A complementary factor relates to the dynamics of occupational structure and the stratification system. In France as in the US (Mendras, 1988; Bell, 1973), the standard hypothesis of stratification change suggests that the long-term educational expansion of the twentieth century, and the emergence of a knowledge-based society, have stimulated the enlargement of the middle and upper-middle classes; thus, the newer generation could have mechanically benefited from the expansion of the occupational groups of experts, managers, or professionals (*"cadres et professions intellectuelles supérieures,"* in French[3]), to whom we often add middle management and lower professionals in the private and public sectors (such as school teachers and nurses), who exemplify the "new technical middle class," whose social hegemony was predicted in the seventies (*"professions intermédiaires"* in the official French nomenclature of occupations).

At the aggregated level, the expansion of these middle and higher occupational groups in France seems to be a demonstration of that idea: for the aggregated age group between thirty and fifty-four, the rise is from 14 percent in 1970 to 26 percent of the total population (Figure 9.2). However, when we make a distinction between age groups, the dynamics are much more complicated: at age thirty, the percentage of those in middle and higher white-collar occupational groups jumped from 14 percent to 23 percent from 1965 to 1975, and reached 24.5 percent in 1980. In the earlier period, the trend strongly accelerated for these "juniors," but stalled after 1980: a 1.5-point increase in the two decades between 1980 and 2000, compared to a 9-point increase in the 1970s.

In the middle of the "Trente glorieuses," France experienced a dramatic expansion of the public sector and high-tech large companies (Airbus, France Télécom, civil nuclear electricity planning,

Figure 9.2
"Cadres et professions intellectuelles supérieures" Plus "Professions
intermédiaires" in Two Age Groups

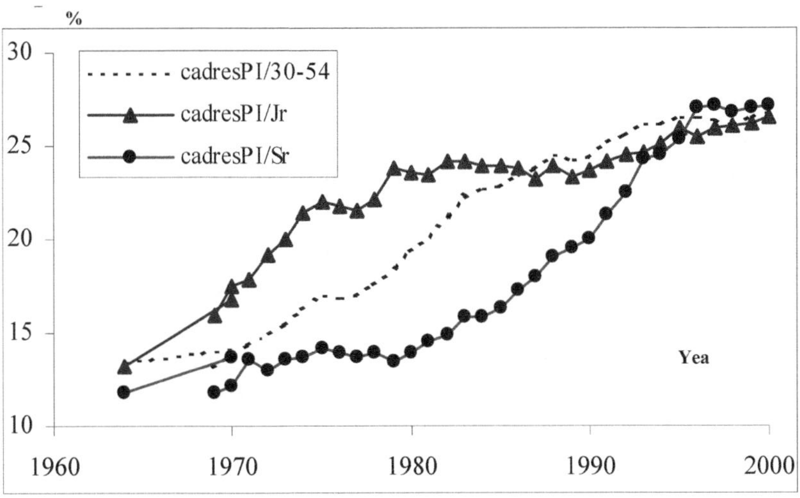

Source: Enquêtes Emploi 1969-2000 et Formation-qualification-professionnelle 1964 et
1977, INSEE; archives LASMAS-Quételet
Note: In 2000, 26 percent of "juniors" (= age group thirty to thirty-four) are in the middle
or higher occupational groups; the figure for seniors (= fifty to fifty-four) is 27 percent.
The proportions were respectively 24.5 percent and 14 percent in 1980. The percentages
are calculated using the total age group population.

health system, universities, and research centers, etc.), creating
strong demand for highly qualified employees with higher education. The first cohorts of the baby boom (the 1945 cohort, which
was thirty years old in 1975) were surely not a sacrificed generation
since they enjoyed longer education in the context of a dynamic
labor market, and did not face the diminishing returns to education
that subsequent cohorts have faced. In 2000, twenty-five years later,
the proportion of thirty-year-olds in mid-level and higher white-
collar occupational groups is quite similar and stable (26 percent),
compared to 23 percent in 1975 and 24.5 percent in 1980. In this
respect, the cohort born in 1970 knows no clear progress. However,
during the 1990s, the expansion for "seniors" (that is, the "juniors"
of the seventies) is obvious. Thus, the expansion of mid-level and
higher occupational groups' across generations is not linear. The
apparent linear growth results from the inappropriate aggregation of

a strong expansion—for the early baby boomers—and of a strong slowdown for the succeeding generations.

Scarring Effect

These evolutions would have had no significant social impact if, for the new generations, these early difficulties had no permanent effect. If the new entrants in the labor force in a period of scarcity could catch up from their early difficulties later in their lives, the problem would be anecdotal or residual. The assessment of the long-term impact of these early difficulties is central to the interpretation; if young, deprived generations do not catch up, a kind of long-term *hysteresis* effect appears that we can call a "scar" or "scarring effect," since the handicap seems definitive. The age-period-cohort analysis shows that cohorts who experienced a difficult (favorable) entry because of a context of recession (expansion) continue to suffer (benefit) from a relative delay (advancement) in upward mobility when they are compared to the average situation. The relative position of a collective cohort at age thirty is rapidly crystallized, and there does not appear to be a substantial catch-up effect later on (Figure 9.3).

How can we explain the lack of a generational catch-up dynamics? Those who had benefited from a period of entry marked by a strong demand for skilled jobs experienced faster career and earlier labor experience at higher levels of responsibility, with better wages; these individuals (and the cohort they constitute at an aggregated level) retain the long term benefits of the early opportunities they enjoyed, which will positively influence their future trajectory at any later age. For those who entered the labor market under difficult economic conditions, the periods of unemployment they faced, the necessity to accept less qualified jobs with lower wages, and the consecutive delays in career progression, imply negative *stimuli* for their own trajectories (decline in ambition, lack of valued work experiences) and could appear as a negative signal for future potential employers. The hypothesis we present here for France is that cohort-specific socialization contexts imply long-term opportunities and life chances for individuals and for their cohorts; when the difficulties disappear, the cohorts who faced

Figure 9.3
Proportion of Service Class Positions *(cadres et professions intermédiaires)* **by Age and Cohort: Cohort Diagram**

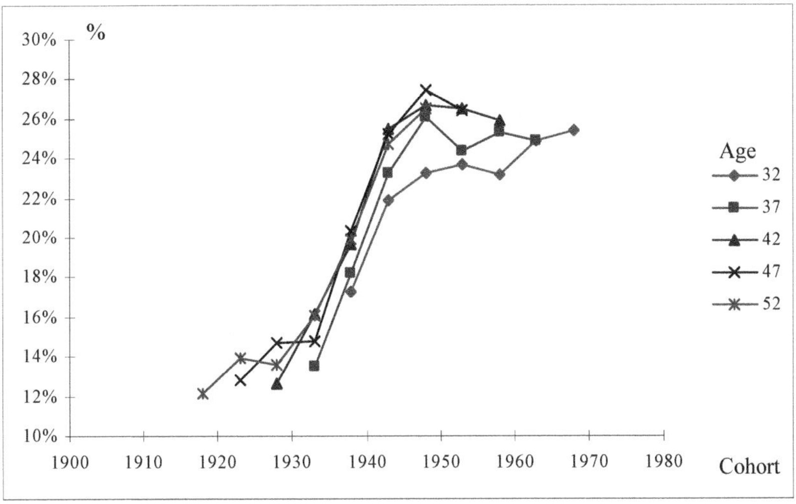

Source: compilation Enquêtes FQP—Enquêtes Emploi (1964-2000).

Note: The cohort diagram is a strong instrument for the analysis of cohort effects. It compares the achievement at the same age of different cohorts. If the curves are linear, we have a stable progress by cohort. If we see cohort accelerations and decelerations affecting the same cohorts, we can analyze long-term cohort effects. The 1948 cohort benefits from an acceleration of its position at age thirty-two (23 percent compared to 17 percent for the 1938 cohort, and less than 12 percent for the 1933 cohort—as we can suppose). The 1958 cohort, which at age thirty-two stalls relative to the 1948 one, does not catch up by age forty-two. At age thirty-two, the rate for the cohort 1968 was two points higher than that of the 1948 one, whereas the rate for the 1948 cohort was about thirteen points higher compared to that of the 1928 cohort. Since the opportunity for growth is neither similar nor linear from one cohort to another, some benefit from better careers than others. Generational history is not linear.

these problems continue to suffer from long-term consequences of past handicaps.

In more concrete terms, the cohorts born during the forties, who benefited from the economic acceleration of the late sixties, were relatively privileged compared to the previous cohorts when young and are relatively advantaged when compared to the newer ones because of the lack of progress for the young from 1975 to the present. We can generalize this observation: the cohorts who entered the labor force after 1975 and experienced an economic slump and mass unemployment have been the early victims of the new generational dynamics, and they retain the long-term scars of their initial difficulties in the labor market.

An important point we cannot develop at length here is the consequences of educational expansion. If the level of education has increased in the cohorts born in 1950 to 1975, that positive trend was accompanied by a strong social devalorization of grades (Chauvel, 2000). More specifically, the first cohorts of the baby boom have benefited from an expansion of education at a time when the rewards to education remained stable: even if there were twice as many *Baccalauréat* recipients in the 1948 cohort than in the 1935 one, their likelihood of access to higher social or economic positions did not shrink. On the other hand, the generations that followed had to deal with a strong trend of devaluation in terms of the economic and social returns to education. The first conse-quence is a rush to the most valued and selective grades (in the *"Grandes écoles"* of the elite such as *Ecole Polytechnique, Ecole Nationale d'Administation, Sciences-Po Paris*, etc.) whose value remains stable, but whose population becomes more and more specific and may be discriminatory in terms of social origins. The second consequence is a strong devalorization of less prestigious universities, which are less exclusive but have much smaller per capita endowments in comparison to the *Grandes écoles*. In the same way, the best secondary schools become more selective with major consequences in terms of urban segregation. In the French case, the school system was traditionally the central institution of the republic and at the heart of its idea of progress, providing the strongest support for French-style social democracy and meritoc-racy. The collapse of the value of grades implies a destabilization of this myth and a pessimistic outlook on progress—developments that we can expect to have political consequences.

Now that we are nearing the end of this long-term slowdown, which began twenty-five years ago, we can compare two social and genealogical generations[4]. For the first time in a period of peace, the youth of the new generation are not better off than their par-ents at the same age. In fact, the "1968 generation," born in 1948, are the children of those born in 1918 who were young adults in World War II and worked in difficult conditions at the beginning of the "*Trente glorieuses.*" The condition of the baby boomers was incomparably better than their parents'. But the following genealogical generation, born around 1978—that is now between twenty-five and thirty years old—faces diminished opportunities of growth, not only because of an economic slump, but also because of their relatively poor outcomes in comparison to those of their own parents who did very well.[5] We now observe rising rates of downward social mobility connected to the proliferation of middle-class children who cannot find social positions comparable to their parents.

Consequently, France offers an ideal typical example of a failure of a corporatist regime, since it is unable to distribute its benefits to young adults, since it sacrifices the interests of large fractions of its population, and since it is unable to organize its own transmission to newer generations. This case is very interesting, indeed, since we have with France a country presenting specific traits: France is defined by an homogeneous culture, notably by a political culture of refusal of market rules; it is homogeneously governed by a centralized system of governance about to produce for long periods the same erroneous diagnoses and decisions on the totality of the territory; it is based on a culture of stop-and-go policies of alternate periods of excessive investments and of scarcity, about to create backlashes and counter-backlashes. France is also a country where the first years on the labor market are strategic for future life-chances of individuals: early successes or early failures become respectively positions of rent or conversely lifelong handicaps. France could be an exception about to experience exceptional inter-cohort inequalities. More decentralized countries (like the United States or Italy) could blur these fractures; more responsible political regimes could avoid stop-and-go policies or accept more rapidly the diagnosis of previous mistakes and act to balance them. Societies where the life course is characterized by more instability or by less conservative processes than in France could be more propitious to redistribution of opportunities between cohorts.

Is France an Exception? An International Comparison of Cohorts

A solution to test this idea of a possible French exceptionalism is to compare the dynamics of incomes on the life course in contrasted nations. Four countries will be considered here: France, Italy, Denmark, and the United States. This choice gives one country by typical welfare regime. The four countries are characterized by similar levels of development and the trends are roughly parallel, even if the behavior of the American economy was somehow better during the 1990's (Figure 9.4).

The four selected countries pertain to samples of micro-data available in the *Luxembourg Income Study Project* (www.lisproject.org), but other typical countries could have been selected with consistent results. Since in this chapter the major concern is about consumption, the focus will be on household level standards of living and not on personal earnings. The LIS project data offers

Figure 9.4
Annual Per Capita GDP of Four Countries (in PPP $ Purchasing Power Parity Dollars)

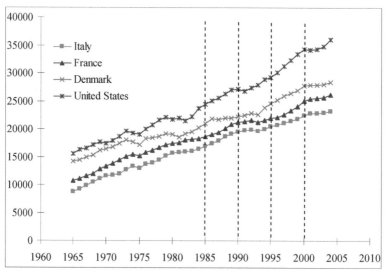

Source: Penn World Tables 6.2 (Heston and et al., 2006). Dotted lines refer to the four periods of the analysis.

the possibility to compute adjusted disposable income (total net income after taxes and transfers, adjusted by household size, where the equivalence scale is the square-root of the number of residents of the household) in order to compare the living standards of age groups at four different periods, respectively around 1985, 1990, 1995, and 2000.

The main results of the comparison of the relative adjusted disposable income (RADI, Figure 9.5) are:

- In 2000, the shapes of the age distribution of the average RADI are similar with an ascending slope to age fifty-five and a declining standard of living after (decline of earnings or retirement).
- From 1985 to 2000, except in the United States, we note a general increase of the senior's income, more modest in Denmark and very significant in France.
- France and Italy are characterized by a strong relative decline of the age group thirty-five to thirty-nine; the French dynamics pertain to a

Figure 9.5
Relative Adjusted Disposable Income (RADI) by Age Group for Three Periods

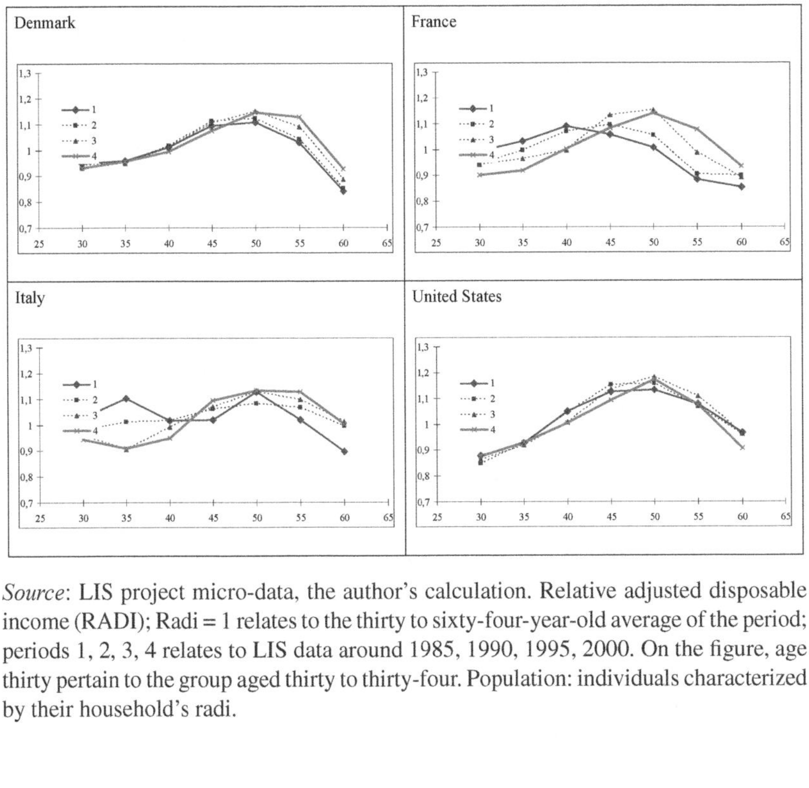

Source: LIS project micro-data, the author's calculation. Relative adjusted disposable income (RADI); Radi = 1 relates to the thirty to sixty-four-year-old average of the period; periods 1, 2, 3, 4 relates to LIS data around 1985, 1990, 1995, 2000. On the figure, age thirty pertain to the group aged thirty to thirty-four. Population: individuals characterized by their household's radi.

very clear cohort wave (there is a progressive shift of age at maximum income from age forty to age fifty).

- In Italy, the decline of RADI at age thirty is less significant, but note that at age thirty most Italians are not head of their own household, and most of them continue to nominally benefit from the affluence of their own seniors.

The main point is that France and Italy show profound redistributions of living standards to the profit of seniors and at the expense of younger, mid-aged adults when Denmark and the United States face no massive transformations (the relative consequences of the slight improvement for Danish seniors is shared by all the other age groups). When both the Nordic and Liberal welfare regimes are about to smoothen inter-cohort inequalities, the corporatist and the familialistic regimes generate visible imbalances between age groups, the age groups relating to the part of the life course when young families appear are marked by profound transformations. In France, when the gap in 1985 between the fifty-five year old and the thirty-five year old age group was down 15 percent, the gap is plus 16 percent in 2000, and we have a redistribution of thirty-one points; in Italy, the numbers are respectively negative 8 percent and plus 22 percent, with a redistribution of thirty points. These implicit redistributions between age groups are not negligible: here is the evidence of the stability of both the Nordic and the Liberal regimes in terms of inter-cohort inequality and of the strong inter-cohort inequalities created inside both the corporatist and the familialistic regimes.

If the inter-cohort inequality dynamics produce different shapes inside the different welfare regimes, intra-cohort inequality matters too. In terms of contrasts between the top and the bottom of the standard of living distribution, the cohort dynamics matter. We measure here the intra-cohort inequality with the inter-decile ratio D9/D1, the ratio between the income of the richest 10 percent and the income of the poorest 10 percent (Figure 9.6).

The most noticeable results are:

- The spectrum of inequality measures is well known: the United States is the most unequal country with Denmark being the most equal; Italy is closer to the United States and France to Denmark.

Figure 9.6
RADI Inequality Measure (Interdecile Ratio)

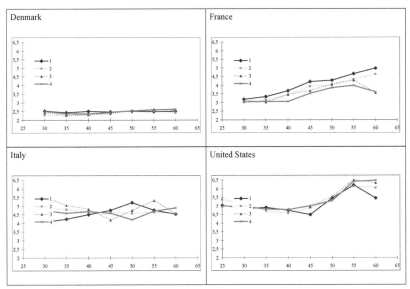

Source: LIS project micro-data, the author's calculation. See previous figure.

- In Denmark, the situation is stable.
- In France, we have a decline in seniors' inequality: in the eighties, the older, the stronger the intra-cohort inequality, and the former older cohorts has been replaced by younger ones which are more equal, but the youngest cohort do not improve their degree of intra-cohort equality.
- The United States faces stronger intra-cohort inequality for seniors (the young being more equal, and inequalities seeming to increase with age), and this structure of increasing inequalities of elders is increasing (the contrast between juniors and seniors is deeper nowadays).
- Italy is more unstable, but younger cohorts face stronger intra-cohort inequality in 2000 than in the mid-1980s when it is the opposite at age fifty. Relatively poorer (Figure 9.5) and more unequal, and dynamically facing pauperization and increasing inequality, the younger Italian cohorts are visibly challenged. Moreover, a deeper analysis (Chauvel, 2007) shows that these elements are even more severe when we include a demographic argument. The situation of young Italian adults is difficult but their answer to this challenge has been a decline in their fertility: less children mean higher standards of living (because the income is shared between less consumption units). If the fertility rate of contemporary young adults remained unchanged when compared to the 1980's, their economic difficulty would be even stronger.

In France, and even more in Italy, the conditions and the standards of living of younger cohorts are destabilized. The young experience dynamics which are significantly less propitious than their elders are. It means a rupture in the welfare regime which is not sustainable, since the socialization of newer cohorts differs from that of previous cohorts, at the expense of newer cohorts.

At the opposite, no radical changes appear in both the Danish and the American dynamics; here are stable welfare regimes with no clear rupture in the process of socialization of different cohorts. The strong social protection in Denmark remains a collective good shared by all age groups, and the American in-egalitarian system remains almost the same on the period 1985-2000 (but if we come back to the previous period of "Reaganomics," the rupture of regime was obvious but is now a question of long-term historical change).

Welfare Regime Ruptures and Consumption

The main conclusion is that the answers of the different welfare regimes to the economic slow down of the post 1970s period differs substantially. The Danish model of welfare faced the challenge with a universalistic objective of stabilization and protection of all age groups equally; the young adults are not the specific victims of any kind of retrenchments in the model. At the opposite part of the inequality spectrum, the United States did not diverge from their principle of competitive markets.

Conversely, the French and the Italian answers to the new challenges with a stronger protection and more affluent positions of seniors and more difficulties for the younger cohorts (lower relative income, difficulties in gaining access to economic independence and in entering the job market, and stronger inequality in Italy) creates a paradoxical situation where social democracy seems to improve in the older cohorts while the young are destabilized. The French diagnosis of double victimization of younger generations (victims of both fake liberalism, which give freedom only to those who have the economic means, and fake socialism, which has forgotten the young) is relevant in Italy also.

The central point of my conclusion pertains to the long-term sustainability of welfare regimes. To be stable in the long term, a social system must arrange its own reproduction from one generation to the next. In France and Italy, today's seniors benefit from a large welfare state, but the vast social rights they were able to accumulate were the consequence of their relatively advantaged careers; we assert that the new generations, when they become seniors themselves, will not be able to benefit from the same rights and the large size of the present welfare state will mechanically erode with cohort replacement—since the reproduction of the welfare regime is not ascertained.

In France, where the generational dynamics of the different social strata are parallel if not similar, the major problem is not generational inequalities, but the fact that newer generations heavily support a welfare system that could collapse before they benefit from it. The problem is not stagnation, but lack of preparation in the long term, at the expense of the most fragile population: the young and the recently socialized generations. Here lies the problem of sustainability for the current welfare regime: it appears large, strong, and durable, but its decline is almost certain; the security it offers to seniors is often at the expense of young cohorts facing radical uncertainty.

In the United States, the case is more complicated. For the young generations, the highest classes enjoy exceptionally better positions while the median classes see their fortunes stagnate and the poor are subjected to relative, if not absolute, deprivation. For the moment, this regime is stable and seems durable. At the opposite, the Danish one shows that high standards of protection, equality, and solidarity could be inter-generationally stable too, since newer cohorts benefit from similar conditions and rights than their elders.

The key question is: Will younger generations in France or Italy continue to sustain a system where their social condition is devalued compared to the older generations with no clear prospects of improvement? For the moment, these intergenerational inequalities are accepted, since they are generally unknown, their social visibility is low and their political recognition null. These examples of the corporatist and familialistic impasse show that if we want solidarity, there is no other way than in a universalistic model (similar to the Nordic one) that supports equally the young, the mid-aged, and the elders in a long-term perspective of socialization. In terms of consumption, these results give a better understanding of differences in the national life course perspective of standards of living. In France, compared to the United States, the young generation faces real difficulties, and at the opposite, the nowadays seniors benefit from a specific economic boom and from economic homogenization (more equality). In France, seniors appear attractive targets for marketing products while the young are often framed in terms of social problems. The Italian situation is similar, but the demographic collapse of young generations of adults (less numerous with less children) and their increasing degree of familialistic dependence reduces the degree of immediate visibility of the social problem, but this problem will necessarily appear raising the question of who will care for elders. At the opposite, Denmark seems to be a stable model of development of a universalistic solidaristic regime of collective improvement. The social problems that appear elsewhere (deepening gap between the rich and the poor, accumulation of social problems for the newer generations, destabilization of the young educated middle class, etc.) seem to be relativized and smoothed, and the general atmosphere is more propitious to a social homogeneity and the development of a "wage earner middle class" in a knowledge-based society. While recognizing there are limitations to the welfare regime model approach, this analysis suggests the universalistic welfare regime is sustainable and maintains its own capacity for long-term development.

Notes

1.   I wish to acknowledge the helpful comments and useful questions that I received from Ian Rees Jones, Martin Hyde, Chris Gilleard, and Paul Higgs.
2.   France and the United States both experienced a period of post-war affluence: the American "Golden Age of Capitalism" (Maddison, 1982) and the French "Trente Glorieuses" (Fourastié, 1979), which contrast with the subsequent period of economic slowdown and "diminished expectations" (Krugman, 1992). See, notably: Chauvel, 1998 (second ed., 2002).
3.   The French representation of the social stratification system in terms of occupation is different from the American one; the French tradition is very strong and contributes to a declining but still central "classist" vision of French society, shared

by most social scientists, the media, and social actors. In this respect, the contrast with the US is dramatic. See also Szreter (1993) who develops a comparative view of the difference in the representations of middle-class occupational groups.
4. During the twentieth century, an average age gap of about thirty years separated parents and their children.
5. These parents are about to help their children in different ways with the intensification of *"solidarités familiales"* (transfers and transmissions between generations including financial, in kind, cultural, and material) that Attias-Donfut (2000) describes, but at the collective level, the first and the most efficient *solidarité* would consist of a redistribution of social positions.

References

Attias-Donfut, C. (2000). *"Rapports de générations: transferts intrafamiliaux et dynamique macrosociale."* *Revue française de sociologie*, 41, 4: 643-684
Auerbach, A.J., J. Gokhale, and L.J. Kotlikoff. (1994). "Generational accounting: A meaningful way to evaluate fiscal policy (in Symposia: Generational Accounting)." *The Journal of Economic Perspectives,* 8, 1: 73-94.
Barbier, J.C. and J. Gautié (dir.). (1998). *Les politiques de l'emploi en Europe et aux Etats Unis, Cahiers du CEE.* Paris: PUF.
Becker, H.A. (2000). "Discontinuous Change and Generational Contracts," in S. Arber and C. Attias-Donfut (Eds), *The Myth of Generational Conflict. The Family and State in Ageing Societies* (pp. 114-132). London, New York: Routledge,.
Bell, D. (1973). *Coming of Post-Industrial Society: A Venture in Social Forecasting.* NY: Basic Books.
Bell, L., G. Burtless, T. Smeeding, J. Gornick. (2007). "Failure to Launch: Cross-National Trends in the Transition to Economic Independence." *Lis Working Paper*, 456.
Bennett, M.J., (2000). *When Dreams Came True: the GI Bill and the Making of Modern America.* Washington, D.C.: Brassey's.
Brzinsky-Fay, C. (2007). "Lost in transition? Labour market entry sequences of school leavers in Europe." *European Sociological Review*, 23: 409-422.
Card, D. et T. Lemieux. (2000). "Can falling supply explain the rising return to college for younger men?: A cohort-based analysis." *NBER working paper series*, 7655.
Castel, R. (2003). *From Manual Workers to Wage Laborers: Transformation of the Social Question.* New Brunswick, NJ: Transaction Publishers.
Chauvel L. (1997). *"L'uniformisation du taux de suicide masculin selon l'âge: effet de génération ou recomposition du cycle de vie?"* *Revue française de sociologie*, XXXVIII-4: 681-734.
Chauvel L., (1998) [2ᵉ ed 2002], *Le destin des générations: structure sociale et cohortes en France au xxᵉ siècle,* Paris, Presses Universitaires de France.
Chauvel L. (2000). *"Valorisation et dévalorisation sociale des titres: une comparaison France – Etats-Unis,"* in A. van Zanten (dir.), *L'état de l'école* (pp. 341-352). Paris: La Découverte.
Chauvel, L. (2003). *"Génération sociale et socialisation transitionnelle: Fluctuations cohortales et stratification sociale en France et aux Etats-Unis au xxᵉ siècle.»* *Mémoire d'Habilitation à Diriger des recherches.* Paris: Sciences-Po.
Chauvel L. (2006). "Social Generations, Life Chances and Welfare Regime Sustainability." in Pepper D. Culpepper, Peter A. Hall, and Bruno Palier (Eds), *Changing France: the Politics that Markets Make* (pp. 341-352). Basingstoke, NY: Palgrave Macmillan.
Chauvel L. (2007). *"Generazioni sociali, prospettive di vita e sostenibilità del welfare"* *La Rivista delle Politiche Sociali*, 4(3): 43-72.

Duru-Bellat M., (2006). *L'inflation scolaire: les désillusions de la méritocratie*. Paris : Le Seuil.
Easterlin, R.A. (1961). "The American baby boom in historical perspective," *American Economic Review*, LI, 5: 869-911.
Easterlin, R.A., C.M. Schaeffer, D.J. Maucunovich. (1993). "Will the baby boomers be less well off than their parents? Income, wealth, and family circumstances over the life cycle in the United States." *Population and Development Review*, 19, 3: 497-522.
Esping-Andersen G. (1990). *The Tree Worlds of Welfare Capitalism*. Cambridge: Cambridge University Press.
Esping-Andersen G. (1999). *Social Foundations of Postindustrial Economies*. Oxford: Oxford University Press.
Esping-Andersen, G., with D. Gallie, A. Hemerijck and J. Myles. (2002). *Why We Need a New Welfare State*. Oxford: Oxford University Press.
Estevez-Abe M., T. Iversen and D. Soskice. (2001). "Social Protection and the Formation of Skills: A Reinterpretation of the Welfare State," in P. Hall and D. Soskice (Eds), *Varieties of Capitalism: The Institutional Foundations of Comparative Advantage* (pp. 145-183). Oxford: Oxford University Press.
Ferrera, M. (1996). "The 'Southern Model' of welfare in social Europe." *Journal of European Social Policy*, 1, 6: 17-37.
Fourastié, J. (1979). *Les Trente Glorieuses ou la révolution invisible*. Paris: Fayard.
Freeman, R.B. (1976). *The Overeducated American*. New York: Academic Press.
Hastings, D.W. and L.G. Berry. (1979). *Cohort Analysis: A Collection of Interdisciplinary Readings*. Oxford, OH: Scripps Foundation for Research in Population Problems.
Heller, D.E. (dir.). (2002). *Conditions of Access: Higher Education for Lower Income Students*. Westport, CT: Praeger Publishers.
Heston, A., R. Summers, and B. Aten. (2006). *Penn World Table Version 6.2*. The University of Pennsylvania: Center for International Comparisons of Production, Income and Prices.
Krugman, P.R. (1992). *The Age of Diminished Expectations: US Economic Policy in the 1990s*. Cambridge, MA: MIT Press.
Maddison, A. (1982). *Phases of Capitalist Development*. Oxford: Oxford university press.
Mannheim, K. (1990) (1928). *Le problème des générations*. Paris: Nathan.
Mason, K.O., W.M. Mason, H.H. Winsborough, and W.H. Poole. (1973). "Some methodological issues in cohort analysis of archival data." *American Sociological Review*, 38: 242-258.
Mayer, K. U. (2005). "Life Courses and Life Chances in a Comparative Perspective," in S. Svallfors (Ed.), *Analyzing Inequality: Life Chances and Social Mobility in Comparative Perspective* (pp. 17-55). Palo Alto, CA: Stanford University Press.
Mead M. (1970). *Culture and Commitment; A Study of the Generation Gap*. Garden City, NY: American Museum of Natural History—Natural History Press.
Mendras, H. (1988). *La seconde révolution française: 1965-1984*. Paris: Gallimard.
Mentré F. (1920). *Les générations sociales*. Paris: Éd. Bossard.
Neumark, D. (2000). *On the Job: Is Long Term Employment a Thing of the Past?* New York, Russell Sage Foundation.
Putnam, R. D. (2000). *Bowling Alone: The Collapse and Revival of American Community*. New York: Simon and Schuster.
Ryder, N.B. (1965). "The cohort as a concept in the study of social change." *American Sociological Review*, 30: 843-861.
Szreter, S.R.S. (1993). "The official representation of social classes in Britain, the United States, and France: The professional model and 'les cadres.'" *Comparative Studies in Society and History*, 35, 2: 285-317.

Thernstrom, S. (1973). *The Other Bostonians: Poverty and Progress in the American Metropolis, 1880-1970.* Cambridge, MA: Harvard University Press.

Van De Velde, C. (2008). *Devenir adulte, Sociologie comparée de la jeunesse en Europe.* Paris: Presses Universitaires de France.

Weir, M. (2002). "The American Middle Class and the Politics of Education," in O. Zunz, *Social Contracts Under Stress: The Middle Classes of America, Europe, and Japan at the Turn of the Century.* New York: Russell Sage Foundation.

About the Contributors

Fanny Bugeja is undertaking a PhD at the "Institut d'Etudes Politiques de Paris" (Sciences-Po University, Paris) and at the "Institut national de la statistique et des études économiques" (INSEE). Her main research interest is in generational fracture and comparative inequalities in household expenditure.

Louis Chauvel is professor of sociology at the Insitute d'Etudes Politiques de Paris (Sciences-Po University, Paris) and is the author of *The Destiny of Generations: social structure and cohorts in the 20th century France*. He is also general secretary of the European Sociological Association.

David J. Ekerdt is professor of sociology and director of the Gerontology Center at the University of Kansas. His funded studies of work and retirement have examined the retirement process and its effects on well-being. He is presently conducting research on American workers' changing plans and decisions for retirement and on the ways that people manage and dispose of their possessions in later life. He was editor-in-chief of the *Macmillan Encyclopedia of Aging*, a four-volume, one-million-word work published in 2002. From 1994 to 1997 he served as editor of the *Journal of Gerontology: Social Sciences* and has led committees and tasks forces on publications for the Gerontological Society of America.

Chris Gilleard is the director of psychology and psychotherapies for South West London & St. George's Mental Health NHS Trust. He holds honorary academic positions in the Faculty of Health & Social Care Sciences, St. George's University of London & Kingston University, and in the Centre for Behavioural & Social

Sciences applied to Medicine, University College London. He is the co-author of two books addressing the changing nature of ageing and later life in contemporary Western society—*Cultures of Ageing: Self, Citizen and the Body* (2000) and *Contexts of Ageing: Class, Cohort and Community* (2005).

Paul Higgs is professor of sociology at University College London. He is co-author of *Cultures of Ageing: Self, Citizen and the Body* (2000) and *Contexts of Ageing: Class, Cohort and Community* (2005). He has published widely in both social gerontology and medical sociology. He is an executive committee member of the ISA RC11 (Sociology of Ageing). He has been closely involved with the English Longitudinal Study of Ageing (ELSA) and led an ESRC project with Ian Rees Jones on the historical emergence of the older consumer in the UK. Paul Higgs and Chris Gilleard were finalists for the Gerontological Society of America's Social Gerontology Award in 2007.

Martin Hyde is senior lecturer in sociology at Sheffield Hallam University. He studied at Bristol University and has previously worked at UCL and Imperial College on studies of ageing, including the English Longitudinal Study of Ageing and the From Passive to Active Consumers project. His interests include globalization, labor markets, and ageing.

Ian Rees Jones is professor of sociology at Bangor University. He has published extensively in the field of medical sociology addressing health inequalities, chronic illness, and medical decision making. He is an executive committee member of the ISA RC11 (Sociology of Ageing) and his research with older people focuses on studies of early retirement and health status post-retirement. He currently leads an ESRC funded research project looking at changing inequalities in health and lifestyles in later life.

George P. Moschis is a professor of marketing at Georgia State University, where he is also an Alfred Bernhardt Research Professor and the Director of the Center for Mature Consumer Studies. He founded and has directed the Center, and has been on the Gerontology Faculty of his University for the past 20 years. Dr. Moschis has been a pioneer in developing educational material, including the first of its kind course, Marketing to Older Adults, and six books on the same topic. He has been recognized by both his peers in academics and business practitioners for his contributions to the field of consumer behavior and marketing, and has helped numerous types of organizations worldwide with issues related to generational marketing.

Pat Thane has been professor of contemporary British History, Institute of Historical Research, University of London since October 2002. She was professor of contemporary history at the University of Sussex from 1994 to 2002. Her publications include *The Foundations of the Welfare State* (1982; 1996); *Women and Gender Policies. Women and the Rise of the European Welfare States, 1880s-1950s* (co-edited with Gisela Bock, 1990); *Old Age from Antiquity to Post-Modernity* (co-edited with Paul Johnson, 1998); *Old Age in England. Past Experiences, Present Issues* (2000); *Women and Ageing in Britain since 1500* (co-edited with Lynne Botelho, 2001); and *The Long History of Old Age* (ed., 2005).

Frank Trentmann is professor of history in the School of History, Classics, and Archaeology at Birkbeck College, in the University of London. He was director of the ESRC and AHRC Cultures of Consumption research program, which funded the conference where the contributions to the manuscript were originally presented. His publications include *Consuming Cultures, Global Perspectives* (with John Brewer; 2006) and *Free Trade Nation: Commerce, Consumption and Civil Society* (2008).

Bryan S. Turner was professor of sociology at the University of Cambridge (1998-2005) and is currently professor of sociology in the Asia Research Institute, National University of Singapore. He is the research leader of the cluster on globalization and religion. He edited the *Cambridge Dictionary of Sociology,* published *Vulnerability and Human Rights* for Penn State University Press

(2006) and edited *The New Blackwell Companion to Social Theory* (2008). With June Edmunds he published *Generations Culture and Society* (2002) and edited *Generational Consciousness, Narrative and Politics* (2002), both of which laid the foundation for thinking about consumer society, baby boomers, and social change. His current research in Asia looks at popular religion, piety, and religion as lifestyle.

Christina Victor is professor of social gerontology and health services research at Reading University. Her main research interests are in the areas of health status in later life, social networks, social relationships in later life, and with developing a population perspective on ageing and later life. She has published widely in peer-reviewed journals, has held research grants from a variety of funding sources (including ESRC and the UK Department of Health) and is the author/editor of eight books in the field of ageing and later life including *The Social Context of Ageing* (2005).

Dick Wiggins is professor of quantitative social science and head of the Department of Quantitative Social Science at the Institute of Education, University of London. His methodological interests include the longitudinal analysis of secondary data covering all aspects of the life course, mixed methods, survey design, attitude measurement and sampling methodology, evaluation research, and policy analysis. Substantive research interests span the exploration of structure and agency in the context of ageing, poverty, physical and mental health and well-being, and cross-national differences in quality of life. His current activities include two secondary analysis projects, "Transitions, choices and health in later life" (under the UK's New Dynamics of Ageing program) and a cross-national study on health and poverty (Canadian Social & Humanities Research Council). He is a member of the Medical Research Council's College of Experts and an expert adviser to the Office for National Statistics' Health Variations Group.

Index